Dear Membe

" The general e
delivered a L
majority of 8
referendum/
secured over
vote. We will
a still divided nation – across countries,
regions, families and friends. Humanity
is facing unprecedented challenges, never
has coming together been more important,
and yet, so far, none of our leaders has
facilitated dialogue to unite us. This book
is an attempt to reintroduce the two 'sides'
of the Brexit debate to one another. We,
perhaps naively, hope it will be a precursor
to understanding, compassion and a more
conciliatory politics. We call upon politicians
to recognise the validity of the diverse
views presented here. It is incumbent
on you to address the concerns of us all. "

GraphicDesign&
12 January 2020

At the start of 2020
GraphicDesign& sent each
of the UK's newly elected
MPs a copy of this book.

A GraphicDesign& book

First published in 2020 by
GraphicDesign&
167 Foundling Court
Brunswick Centre
London WC1N 1AN
UK

info@graphicdesignand.com
www.graphicdesignand.com

ISBN 978 0 9572381 5 2

Designed by
LucienneRoberts+

Printed and bound by
CPI (UK) Ltd
Croydon CR0 4YY

Distributed by
Central Books

© GraphicDesign& 2020

The Other Side
a GraphicDesign& Politics title
[WFG& R]

GraphicDesign& is
a pioneering publishing
house dedicated to
creating intelligent, vivid
books that explore how
graphic design connects
with all other things and
the value that it brings.

Established by Lucienne
Roberts and Rebecca Wright,
GraphicDesign& partners
graphic designers with experts
from other fields to inform,
educate, entertain and
provoke – and to challenge
perceptions about what and
who graphic design is for.

www.graphicdesignand.com

10 9 8 7 6 5 4 3 2 1

A CIP catalogue record for
this book is available from
the British Library.

GraphicDesign&

THE OTHER SIDE

REMAIN

An Emotional Map of Brexit Britain

Editors
Lucienne Roberts
Rebecca Wright

Advisors
Nadine Chahine
Ian Leslie
Paul McNeil

Contents
Remain

Lucienne Roberts is director of the London studio LucienneRoberts+, committed to making accessible, engaging work with a socially aware agenda, and co-founder of the design advocacy initiative GraphicDesign&. Studio clients include Wellcome Collection, Royal Academy of Arts and the Design Museum. Lucienne was Typographer-in-Residence 2018 at the Hoffmitz Milken Center for Typography, ArtCenter College of Design, Los Angeles, is a fellow of the Royal Society of Arts and a member of the Alliance Graphique Internationale. Lucienne voted Remain.

Rebecca Wright is a design educator and writer, Dean of Academic Programmes at Central Saint Martins, University of the Arts, London, and co-founder of the design advocacy initiative GraphicDesign&. She lectures and acts as a consultant at academic institutions across the UK and abroad, is a D&AD trustee and was vice president of ico-D, the International Council of Design, 2015–17. Rebecca voted Remain.

Lucienne and Rebecca were among *Creative Review* magazine's 50 Creative Leaders of 2017.

Nadine Chahine is a Lebanese type designer and former UK type director of Monotype, where she was also legibility expert and Arabic specialist. She has an MA in Typeface Design from Reading University and a PhD from Leiden University, the Netherlands. In 2018 Nadine left Monotype to study for a master's in International Relations at Cambridge University and to develop her foundry ArabicType. Nadine was not eligible to vote in the 2016 UK referendum.

Ian Leslie is an author and commentator on culture, ideas and politics and an expert on communications. His writing has featured in the *Financial Times*, the *Economist* and the *New Statesman*. He co-presents a regular podcast for the RSA, *Polarised*, about the way we do politics today. His latest book on human behaviour, *Why Everybody's Talking and Nobody's Listening*, is on productive disagreement and will be published in 2020. Ian voted Remain.

Paul McNeil is a graphic designer, writer and educator. In 2009 he co-founded MuirMcNeil, with Hamish Muir, a design consultancy focused on exploring systematic methods in design and typography. *The Visual History of Type*, Paul's definitive survey of type design from 1450 to 2015, was published in 2017. He is a member of the International Society of Typographic Designers. Paul voted Remain.

Thank you

To our contributors

This project would not have been possible without our many and varied Leave and Remain contributors, whose thoughts and comments are the making of this book. We thank you for being prepared to take part and for your honesty.

To our advisors

Nadine Chahine
typographer and academic, who helped us explain how important visual communication is

Ian Leslie
author and commentator, who helped us understand how communication really works

Paul McNeil
graphic designer, writer and educator, who helped us explore if neutrality in typography is really possible

To our colleagues and associates

John McGill
designer and all-round GD& supporter, without whom our books could not happen

Sarah Schrauwen
designer and editor, whose energy and commitment keeps it all moving

Sarah Boris, Astrid Stavro
politically engaged graphic designers, who so patiently offered observations that informed our design process

Lorna Fray
editorial advisor, whose insight, knowledge and care has kept us on track

Ruby Buttolph
style-checker, for her eagle-eyed attention to typographic detail

Anabel Navarro
picture researcher, whose meticulous searching has brought the image section to life

and

Daphne Tagg
editor and advisor, who so willingly brought time, talent and thought to this project

To our families

Damian Wayling
Katy Roberts-Wayling
Lawrence Zeegen
Zoë Zeegen
Patrick Wright
Judy Wright

who continue to support us in our long and compelling endeavour

Rebecca Wright would also like to thank Central Saint Martins, University of the Arts London

About this book
Rebecca Wright

In June 2016 the UK held a referendum on its membership of the EU. Leave won with 52 per cent of the vote. GraphicDesign& is among the 48 per cent who voted Remain. As Remainers ourselves, the result was profoundly shocking. So too, the adversarial and divisive rhetoric that has continued unabated in politics and the press ever since. This book was born of our deep frustration and despair at this polarising discourse. We set out to counter it, to get beyond the clichéd stereotypes of Leavers and Remainers, the sound bite and vox pop, by representing the diversity of views held by individual voters and, perhaps more importantly, giving people space to explain the reasons for them.

Our contributors are Leave and Remain voters drawn from around the country, across professions and of diverse ages, backgrounds and perspectives. We include 26 Leavers and 24 Remainers, to reflect the referendum result. We asked that each tell us a little of their life story, how they voted in the 2016 referendum and why. We asked them all to share one loss and one gain they could imagine as a consequence of the 2016 result. Perhaps naively, we thought this process might prompt empathy for 'the other side', but often it did not. Instead, it revealed the huge range and depth of emotion felt by voters – pride, anger, heartbreak, revenge, loneliness, relief, fear, hope.

What it also revealed were multiple failures of communication before, during and after the referendum – the failure of politics to speak for and to communities that felt left behind, failures in communicating the complexity and reality of the EU project, failures in holding politicians to account, and failures to reach out to each other across the divide. These failures have fostered and reinforced division – not least the Remain campaign's failure to understand the need to connect with voters on an emotional level.

As Remainers, we found these failures in communication distressing, as graphic communication designers, we found them perplexing, but they are central to the concept of this GraphicDesign& book. Its design and contents have been conceived to therefore foreground the role of communication in Britain's relationship with Europe. We wanted to give Remain and Leave contributors equal billing, so neither comes first. Instead, the book has two beginnings and no end, with the 'sides' meeting in the middle. If you are only interested in hearing from one side, then this is possible. However, an illustrated essay by typographer Nadine Chahine precedes the Leave contributions and an interview with cultural commentator Ian Leslie prefaces the Remain responses. Our hope is that readers will flip the book over, dip into all the content and listen to what both sides have to say.

There are caveats to what you are about to read. While we found reaching city-dwelling Remainers relatively easy, it was sobering to discover how hard it was for us to find contributors from further across the country, especially those who voted Leave. We are very grateful to our friends of friends of friends who helped us find a more representative cross section of the UK. It is also important to note that we began this project in early 2019, with contributions submitted before the first Brexit deadline of 29 March 2019 (the date received is included alongside each response). The book is therefore a snapshot of a very particular time in British history. Yet despite all that has happened since, our contributors stood by their answers when they checked their proofs in the autumn of 2019.

We are indebted to every one of our contributors for their patience, their interest in this project, and their honesty and generosity in sharing their reflections, opinions and time. It goes without saying that without them this book would not have been possible. And finally, we hope it will be self-evident that this book is not about trying to convert Leave voters. In its design it attempts a different type of communication – person-to-person – to seed understanding, empathy and perhaps even reconciliation.

About the design
Lucienne Roberts

The design of this book is conceived to introduce readers to 'the other side'. It reads in both directions, with Remain contributions reading from one end and Leave from the other. The red, white and blue cover, opened flat, shows two arrows in a flag-like formation. The text pages are black and white only, aside from a short illustrated essay in colour.

Contributor responses run alphabetically by surname. This might be logical, but we wanted the design to signal the variety of voices included and ensure that readers felt happy to dip in and out of the texts at will. So, we decided to identify our contributors typographically. The UK has 12 electoral regions that return members to the European Parliament. We took this as a starting point for various typographic experiments, assigning a different typeface to each region. Employing fonts of contrasting styles inadvertently favoured the reading of one contribution over another, so we opted for typographic neutrality, allocating one sans serif font per MEP region. Intentionally, we selected post-war typefaces only, many epitomising what is known as the 'International Style'.

Our selection was informed by Paul McNeil's book *The Visual History of Type*. He explains more about the history and characteristics of each typeface on pages 022–037. The regional key is shown on page 023.

The Other Side has two front covers. The Remain contributor texts read in one direction, and Leave in the other.

The Remain cover is predominantly blue, Leave is red. The colours interlock in stripes on the spine. There are 12 blue and 13 red stripes to reflect the split in the 2016 vote.

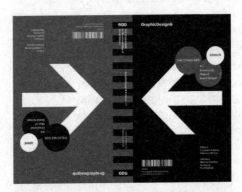

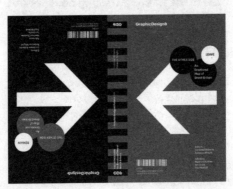

You are currently in the Remain side of the book. 'Telling the other side they are wrong doesn't work,' says communications expert Ian Leslie (below). Look out for the interview with Ian on pages 016–021. 'Leave didn't win because of superior design.' Flip the book over and turn to pages 016–051 to understand the role of visual communication in the UK/Europe story from the 1950s to now (bottom).

DESIGN

Leave and Remain
Communication successes and failures
Ian Leslie

People who study how humans communicate say we operate on two levels: content and relationship. Mostly, we communicate on both levels at the same time. If we are in agreement at the relationship level – I respect you and you respect me, you hear what I'm saying and I hear you – then the content level is going to go a lot better. But often there is some sort of uncertainty or disagreement at the subterranean level, which messes up the content level.

People will be more sensitive to the relationship if their identity is at stake. You might say the failure of the Remain campaign was that they didn't attend to the relationship; they focused on the content and kept hammering away at this. A relationship scientist who studies marriages will say the same thing happens, it's usually men, apparently, who tend to concentrate on the content level as a solution to the relationship level. It's a common mistake. Remain were talking about facts, without addressing that people were saying, 'This relationship is messed up – between us and you, us and London, us and politics: you need to acknowledge that before we can listen to you about whether or not this is good for ODP.' The genius of the Leave campaign was that they went straight for the relationship level. They didn't need to do much on the content level because they understood the relationship was the thing.

INTERVIEW

1952–2016
Yes or No to the European Community

European integration has long divided British politics. When the European Coal and Steel Community was formed in 1952, the UK chose not to be included. The Treaty of Rome created the European Economic Community (EEC, or Common Market) in 1957. This was the precursor to the EU, and the UK again chose not to join it.

Daily Mail
COMMENT
EUROPE. HERE WE COME!

By the 1970s views were shifting. The European project seemed a success, while Britain's economic fortunes had changed. The Conservative government argued for integration. The Labour Party was divided. On 1 January 1973 the UK joined the EEC without holding a referendum.

Daily Mail
1 January 1973
The British press has always had a key role in influencing public opinion. Strongly pro-Brexit (Leave) until late 2016, the Daily Mail were historically pro-European, as this front page shows.

We have used several sans serif typefaces for the contributor responses. Each one represents a different region of the UK. As you are currently in the Remain side of the book you will find the key on page 023 (below).

Turn to pages 024–037 to find out more about the history and characterisitics of each of these sans serifs (bottom). Intentionally, they are all post war, many epitomising what is known as the 'International Style'.

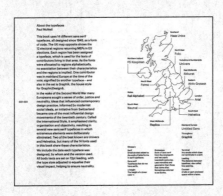

About the typefaces
Paul McNeil

This book uses 14 different sans serif typefaces, all designed since 1945, as a form of code. The UK map opposite shows the 12 electoral regions returning MEPs in EU elections. Each region has been assigned a typeface, which is used for the texts of contributors living in that area. As the fonts were allocated to regions alphabetically, no association between their characteristics and the regions is implied. One contributor was in mainland Europe at the time of the vote, signified by another typeface – and also in the set is Graphik, the house style for GraphicDesign&.

In the wake of the Second World War many Europeans sought a sense of order, justice and neutrality, ideas that influenced contemporary design practice. Informed by modernist social ideals, an initiative from Switzerland became one of the most influential design movements of the twentieth century. Called the International Style, it emphasised clarity, organisation and objectivity, resulting in several new sans serif typefaces in which extraneous elements were deliberately eliminated. Two of the best known are Univers and Helvetica, but many of the 14 fonts used in this book share these characteristics.

We include the date each typeface was designed, by whom and the version used. All body texts are set on 12pt leading, with the type sizes adjusted to equalise their visual impact, helping to ensure neutrality.

022–023

Scotland
Haas Unica

North East
Folio

Yorkshire & Humberside
Univers

East Midlands
Akkurat

Eastern
Aktiv Grotesk

London
Arial

South East
Helvetica

Mainland Europe
Untitled Sans

Throughout
Graphik

Northern Ireland
FS Koopman

North West
Forma

Wales
Rail Alphabet

South West
Neutral

West Midlands
Replica

Northern Ireland
FS Koopman

Aware that the contemporary type marketplace is packed with Helvetica clones, Andy Lethbridge and Stuart de Rozario set out to create a sans serif family that was as competent but presented much more warmth and personality. The result is a hybrid combining the reliable utility of the post-war Swiss neo-grotesques, the robust confidence of earlier twentieth-century American gothics, and the eccentric affability of pre-war British grotesques. FS Koopman is a gentle, approachable sans serif with a robust structure and details that are graceful rather than brutally minimal.

024–025

Scotland
Haas Unica

Commissioned by the Haas Foundry in 1974, Unica was developed by Christian Mengelt, André Gürtler and Erich Gschwind. Their ambition, like that of many designers before and since, was to surpass Helvetica, the typeface that had dominated the graphic design industry since its release in 1957. The new design was developed during six years of intensive work, drawing on detailed comparisons of several competing contemporary sans serifs. The result, Haas Unica, the name a compound of Univers and Helvetica, was a restrained type family, warmer than Helvetica and less clinical than Univers, with letter contours that are notable for their careful stroke balance, delicate curves and sharply defined intersections. Haas Unica was not a commercial success: when the Haas foundry closed down, Unica disappeared with it, in the process achieving cult status.

FONTS

014–015

Each contributor has four pages. To emphasise the double-ended design of the book, the horizontal axis of the pages determines the position of the text, with texts rising and falling from this point in equal measure.

The first spread carries biographical information such as age, occupation and region, opposite reasons for the way contributors voted. The second spread shows each contributor's chosen loss and gain from the referendum vote.

DESIGN

Leave and Remain
Communication successes and failures
Ian Leslie

People's Vote march
19 October 2019

According to organisers,
up to a million people
joined this march in London.
A sea of blue and yellow
EU flags, marchers were
calling for a 'final say' on
the terms of the withdrawal
agreement negotiated
by government.

The failure of Remain and the genius of Leave

People who study how humans communicate say we operate on two levels: content and relationship. Mostly, we communicate on both levels at the same time. If we are in agreement at the relationship level – I respect you and you respect me, you hear what I'm saying and I hear you – then the content level is going to go a lot better. But often there is some sort of uncertainty or disagreement at the subterranean level, which messes up the content level.

People will be more sensitive to the relationship if their identity is at stake. You might say the failure of the Remain campaign was that they didn't attend to the relationship; they focused on the content and kept hammering away at this. A relationship scientist who studies marriages will say the same thing happens. It's usually men, apparently, who tend to concentrate on the content level as a solution to the relationship level. It's a common mistake. Remain were talking about facts, without addressing that people were saying, 'This relationship is messed up – between us and you, us and London, us and politics; you need to acknowledge that before we can listen to you about whether or not this is good for GDP.' The genius of the Leave campaign was that they went straight for the relationship level. They didn't need to do much on the content level because they understood the relationship was the thing.

Acknowledging what happened in 2016

A vote forces us to think about the other side. Leave voters sent a very strong message that a lot of Remainers still haven't heard. Remainers have to find a way of saying to Leavers, 'You were right,' about something. It might be, 'You were right to want to leave the EU, therefore we'll compromise and get out on a deal' – that's one position. Another position would be to say, 'Let's just hold off on doing a deal as there is a lot we haven't thought through yet, but we do want to say you were right about these other things...' What Remainers can't say – and what it sounds like they are saying to a lot of Leavers – is, 'It's all rubbish, you were duped and we are going to erase this.'

Remainers have to find a way to show that they have heard that something has to change. The first principle of a Remain political argument should be to acknowledge something very important happened in 2016. It can't be ignored.

How to build communication between Leavers and Remainers

It's hard, but telling the other side they are wrong doesn't work. This is an insight drawn from addiction counselling – the more you tell an addict to stop drinking or smoking, the more they will want to carry on. So, we have to resist this righting-reflex. We all have it, whether we're talking to our children or somebody on Twitter. If we think they're wrong, we want to put them right. With political arguments it immediately becomes a push-pull situation. This approach very rarely changes someone's mind or enriches discussion.

We have an innate desire to be free, and the moment we feel insecure and that someone is pressurising us, we push back. A change in the equilibrium is more likely if there is respect for the other person and interest in them. But this is the thing – terrorist interrogators, hostage negotiators, addiction counsellors all say it – you can't fake it. It has to be a genuine interest in the other person.

Moving beyond Leave and Remain as different sides

There is a problem in identifying as either a Remainer or a Leaver. Once an opinion or belief becomes part of one's identity, it becomes harder to change. We need to try and put aside Remain and Leave and make arguments that don't depend on sides. An effective Remain campaign should remind us that the EU was not very important to most people until the referendum.

I think the one argument that might unite people is that there are more important things to worry about. Isn't it better to spend the money on the NHS? We should be recruiting teachers and nurses, not diplomats and lawyers and civil servants to engage in these endless negotiations – this country has bigger problems. I think this would be a much more powerful argument than trying to persuade people to stay in the EU, which many people would react against.

Understanding communication as a feedback loop

Cybernetics is an underrated strand of post-war thinking that emerged from a cross-disciplinary group that included anthropologists and technologists who were trying to work out what it means to communicate. The idea of feedback loops came from cybernetics. I find it a really useful way to think about conversations and arguments. We are not just exchanging a series of messages back and forth. What we say and how we say it affects the way someone will respond. If you start showing you're irritated, you are immediately making it happen in them too. I think we need to understand communication as a feedback loop not just as an exchange of messages.

I think we treat a lot of our big arguments like they are finite games, when actually we should be thinking how we could make them infinite. Leave or Remain, we all have to live together and we are going to have to find a way of turning this into a game that we want to keep playing.

INTERVIEW

GraphicDesign& were in conversation with Ian on 18 March 2019.

About the typefaces
Paul McNeil

This book uses 14 different sans serif typefaces, all designed since 1945, as a form of code. The UK map opposite shows the 12 electoral regions returning MEPs in EU elections. Each region has been assigned a typeface, which is used for the texts of contributors living in that area. As the fonts were allocated to regions alphabetically, no association between their characteristics and the regions is implied. One contributor was in mainland Europe at the time of the vote, signified by another typeface – and also in the set is Graphik, the house style for GraphicDesign&.

In the wake of the Second World War many Europeans sought a sense of order, justice and neutrality, ideas that influenced contemporary design practice. Informed by modernist social ideals, an initiative from Switzerland became one of the most influential design movements of the twentieth century. Called the International Style, it emphasised clarity, organisation and objectivity, resulting in several new sans serif typefaces in which extraneous elements were deliberately eliminated. Two of the best known are Univers and Helvetica, but many of the 14 fonts used in this book share these characteristics.

We include the date each typeface was designed, by whom and the version used. All body texts are set on 12pt leading, with the type sizes adjusted to equalise their visual impact, helping to ensure neutrality.

Scotland
Haas Unica

North East
Folio

Northern Ireland
FS Koopman

Yorkshire & Humberside
Univers

East Midlands
Akkurat

Eastern
Aktiv Grotesk

North West
Forma

London
Arial

Wales
Rail Alphabet

South West
Neutral

South East
Helvetica

West Midlands
Replica

Mainland Europe
Untitled Sans

Throughout
Graphik

Glossary

Serif
Small strokes added to the ends of letterforms in serif typefaces.

Sans serif
Typefaces that do not have serifs.

x-height
The height of a lower case 'x'.

Grotesque
Style of sans serif from the nineteenth and very early twentieth centuries. Less monoline and geometric than those that came after. Sometimes referred to as Gothic.

Terminal
Any stroke which does not terminate in a serif.

Leading
The distance between baselines, also called line-spacing.

Counter
A fully or part-enclosed space within a letter.

Throughout
Graphik

Graphik was designed to be a multipurpose tool. Designer Christian Schwartz wanted to develop an extensive type system that would suit the broadest range of possible expressions in the broadest range of possible contexts. He didn't want to reference post-war modernist fonts, such as Helvetica and Univers, and instead drew inspiration from several less well-used twentieth-century sans serifs such as Plak, Folio and Neuzeit Grotesk. The outcome is an extensive, versatile type system based on a rational approach to weights, widths and styles. Its plain but adaptable personality allows Graphik to be the central feature of a design or to play a supporting role in a wide range of typographic environments.

2009
Christian Schwartz
USA
Version/weight used:
Graphik Medium
9pt/12pt
Word spacing 90%
Letter spacing 0%

East Midlands
Akkurat

Laurenz Brunner's Akkurat typeface strikes a balance between tradition and modernity by reconciling the rational qualities of post-war typefaces like Helvetica and Univers with the charming idiosyncrasies of older grotesques from the early twentieth century. Akkurat combines a sober, compact appearance with an inviting personality, seen in features such as the double-storeyed g and the hooked tails of the lower case a and l. On its release in 2004, Akkurat immediately became the font of choice for graphic designers who were keen to revive an expression of modern values in their work.

FONTS

2004
Laurenz Brunner
Switzerland
Version/weight used:
Akkurat Regular
9.25pt/12pt
Word spacing 90%
Letter spacing –1%

Eastern
Aktiv Grotesk

Bruno Maag intended Aktiv Grotesk to be
a viable alternative to Helvetica, a typeface
which he has reviled as the 'vanilla ice cream'
of the designer's type library. Aktiv Grotesk
does not include any of the quirky references
to nineteenth-century grotesques that
are found in other recent sans serif revivals.
Instead, like Helvetica, it was designed to
be simple, consistent and clear, providing
an authoritative but self-effacing alternative
that can lend any message a confident tone
of voice without shouting. It is distinguished
by the angled cut of the upper terminals
of rounded characters, which contrasts with
the horizontal trim of the lower terminals.

2010–2018
Bruno Maag
Switzerland
Version/weight used:
Aktiv Grotesk Regular
9pt/12pt
Word spacing 100%
Letter spacing 0%

London
Arial

Arial is a default font in most personal computers, instantly familiar to anyone who uses one. It is commonly thought that it was originally commissioned by Microsoft. In fact, it was made for another computer giant, IBM, by a team at Monotype led by Robin Nicholas. In order to substitute the new typeface for Helvetica without changing the length of text columns, all of Arial's widths and spaces were configured to match Helvetica's precisely. With contours drawn from an older design from 1926, Monotype Grotesque, Arial's warm and familiar appearance can largely be attributed to the curves on letters such as c and s that terminate at natural angles in relation to the stroke rather than being severed abruptly at horizontals or verticals.

1982
Robin Nicholas
United Kingdom
Version/weight used:
Arial Regular
9.1pt/12pt
Word spacing 85%
Letter spacing 0%

North East
Folio

Folio was released in 1957, the same year as
Helvetica and Univers. It is, however, modelled
more closely on traditional nineteenth-century
grotesques. The intention of its designers,
Konrad Bauer and Walter Baum, was to
develop a rational typeface that improved
on the nineteenth-century sans serif form
by smoothing out some of its more eccentric
attributes. It features a smaller x-height than
Helvetica or Univers, along with a subtler
stroke contrast that becomes increasingly
evident in heavier weights. Although it was both
innovative and systematic, Folio has always
been overshadowed by Helvetica and Univers,
the two bestselling typefaces that have
continued to dominate the sans serif market.

1957
Konrad Bauer and
Walter Baum
Germany
Version/weight used:
Folio Light
9.5pt/12pt
Word spacing 95%
Letter spacing 0%

North West
Forma

Forma was developed for the Nebiolo type foundry by a group of eminent Italian designers led by Aldo Novarese. Lacking any contemporary sans serif designs in its catalogue, the project was driven by Nebiolo's urgent need to compete with the hugely successful sans serifs of the day, such as Helvetica and Univers. Aiming to achieve a perfect alphabet, Forma's designers undertook an exhaustive research and development process involving a comprehensive series of legibility tests together with comparative analysis of several competing sans serif designs. Forma is distinguished by tightly set contours that are finely modulated, with strokes that flare outwards almost imperceptibly at terminals, giving it a much crisper appearance than most sans serif designs.

FONTS

1965–1968
Aldo Novarese
Italy
Version/weight used:
Forma DJR Regular
9pt/12pt
Word spacing 110%
Letter spacing 2%

Northern Ireland
FS Koopman

Aware that the contemporary type marketplace is packed with Helvetica clones, Andy Lethbridge and Stuart de Rozario set out to create a sans serif family that was as competent but presented much more warmth and personality. The result is a hybrid combining the reliable utility of the post-war Swiss neo-grotesques, the robust confidence of earlier twentieth-century American gothics, and the eccentric affability of pre-war British grotesques. FS Koopman is a gentle, approachable sans serif with a robust structure and details that are graceful rather than brutally minimal.

2018
Andy Lethbridge
Stuart de Rozario
United Kingdom
Version/weight used:
FS Koopman Regular
9.5pt/12pt
Word spacing 100%
Letter spacing 0%

Scotland
Haas Unica

Commissioned by the Haas Foundry in 1974, Unica was developed by Christian Mengelt, André Gürtler and Erich Gschwind. Their ambition, like that of many designers before and since, was to surpass Helvetica, the typeface that had dominated the graphic design industry since its release in 1957. The new design was developed during six years of intensive work, drawing on detailed comparisons of several competing contemporary sans serifs. The result, Haas Unica, its name a compound of Univers and Helvetica, was a restrained type family, warmer than Helvetica and less clinical than Univers, with letter contours that are notable for their careful stroke balance, delicate curves and sharply defined intersections. Haas Unica was not a commercial success: when the Haas foundry closed down, Unica disappeared with it, in the process achieving cult status.

FONTS

1980
Christian Mengelt,
André Gürtler and
Erich Gschwind
Switzerland
Version/weight used:
LL Unica 77 Regular
9.1pt/12pt
Word spacing 100%
Letter spacing 0%

South East
Helvetica

Helvetica unarguably qualifies as a design
'classic'. Originally designed in 1957, it
was rationalised by Linotype in 1983 as
a coordinated system with a huge number
of weights and variants and renamed Neue
Helvetica. Bundled with personal computers
since the late 1980s, it is one of the few
typefaces that are now as well known to
the general public as they are to members
of the design community. Because it has few
idiosyncrasies in its letterforms and no features
that might suggest any specific historical
reference points, Helvetica has been used
by many businesses and corporations seeking
to appear modern, authoritative and neutral.
As a result, it is seen everywhere today.

1957
Max Miedinger
Switzerland
Version/weight used:
Neue Helvetica Regular
9.1pt/12pt
Word spacing 90%
Letter spacing 0%

South West
Neutral

Kai Bernau's Neutral is the result of an
academic research project looking at whether
it is possible to create an invisible typeface,
a design so free of stylistic associations
that its design doesn't influence the reading
of a text at all. Bernau measured and averaged
the character sets from the most successful
twentieth-century sans serif typefaces,
basing the construction of his new font on
these mathematical parameters. The result,
a design infused by the DNA of its many
ancestors, provides evidence that, while
conventional notions of beauty may depend
on archetypes and norms, and while self-
effacement may have a place in certain
typographic contexts, there is no such thing
as neutrality.

FONTS

2005–2014
Kai Bernau
Germany
Version/weight used:
Neutral Regular
8.7pt/12pt
Word spacing 90%
Letter spacing 0%

Wales
Rail Alphabet

Jock Kinneir and Margaret Calvert are revered
for their innovative Transport Alphabet, used
for road signage throughout the UK since 1957.
In contrast, Kinneir/Calvert's Rail Alphabet
was designed to be used on public signage
in pedestrian environments. Originally drawn
in two versions as components in a coordinated
signage system, it first appeared in the UK's
NHS hospitals and was subsequently adopted
by British Rail as part of a rebrand for station
signage, trackside signs, notices, signs in trains
and train liveries. It was later used by both the
British Airports Authority and Danish Rail. As
a design, Rail Alphabet shares so many features
with the bold weight of Helvetica that they are
almost indistinguishable, although not identical.

1965
Jock Kinneir and
Margaret Calvert
United Kingdom
Version/weight used:
New Rail Alphabet
Medium
8.75pt/12pt
Word spacing 100%
Letter spacing 0%

West Midlands
Replica

Replica's supple appearance obscures the
mathematical reductivism underpinning its
construction. Dimitri Bruni and Manuel Krebs
from design studio Norm frequently prescribe
strict rules as the starting points for their
projects. In the design of Replica, they
determined the formation of its characters
by means of a rigorously simple grid. In
drawing the letterforms, Bruni and Krebs
then used a variety of local compensatory
techniques to overcome the grid's limits and
to realise a remarkably well-balanced typeface
with a soft, low-contrast appearance. To
achieve a coherently soft contour, all external
and internal stroke junctions in Replica are
bevelled, creating a slightly swollen impression
within counter forms.

FONTS

2008
Dimitri Bruni and
Manuel Krebs
Switzerland
Version/weight used:
Replica Regular
9.35pt/12pt
Word spacing 90%
Letter spacing 0%

Yorkshire & Humberside
Univers

Univers is a landmark in the history of typography, the first type family constructed as a cohesive system with a strict modular framework from the outset. Combining rationality with elegant expressiveness, it was drawn by the prodigious Swiss type designer Adrian Frutiger while he was working for the Deberny & Peignot foundry in France. Like Helvetica, released in the same year, Univers is modelled on the archetypal forms of nineteenth-century grotesques but is more severe than any of its competitors, with every superfluous feature excised, resulting in a design that is unobtrusive and exceptionally versatile. The stiff geometries found in many competing twentieth-century sans serifs are replaced with subtle, slightly squared arcs. Vertical and horizontal strokes are also consistently terminated, either horizontally or vertically, to give a resolute quality to each letterform.

1954–1957
Adrian Frutiger
Switzerland
Version/weight used:
Univers 55
9.1pt/12pt
Word spacing 90%
Letter spacing –1%

Mainland Europe
Untitled Sans

Kris Sowersby, of the Klim type foundry, developed Untitled Sans by cannibalising one of his earlier typefaces, National. Finding the earlier design too expressive and too formal, he started rationalising and simplifying the letterforms, aiming for an idealised typeface of sorts that was as unrecognisable and as plain as it was functional. Taking inspiration from the design philosophies of Jasper Morrison and Naoto Fukusawa, over several years Sowersby drew and redrew letterforms without any immediate historical or visual references in an attempt to remove any identifiable trace of the human hand or individuality. He has described the result, Untitled Sans, as the typographic equivalent of muzak: you don't have to think about it too hard but it is enormously useful.

2013–2017
Kris Sowersby
New Zealand
Version/weight used:
Untitled Sans Regular
9.1pt/12pt
Word spacing 100%
Letter spacing 0%

We asked 24 Remainers to tell us a little of their life story, why they voted the way they did, and to cite one loss and one gain they could imagine following the 2016 result.

Contributors

REMAIN

Darren Bray

              black cab driver
              49
     born   Barking
 educated   GCSEs,
Mayesbrook Comprehensive,
              Dagenham
   living   Hornchurch, Essex
  working   London

text received 16 February 2019

I left school in 1985 with four GCSEs. My school careers advice was to join the army or work at the nearby Ford factory. I didn't want to do either, so I studied the Knowledge.

My main reason for voting Remain was that not one expert or commentator on the Leave side could convince me that my family would be better off outside the EU. Cutting ourselves off seemed very shortsighted. I know there have been objections to our membership of the EU since the 1970s; however, if we were going to leave, the withdrawal should have been better thought out. From 2008 the austerity measures following the collapse of the financial markets (which, incidentally, has cost the British tax payer in the region of a trillion pounds) have affected everyone's day-to-day lives. On top of a decade of cuts in public services, a small group of wealthy individuals from the Leave campaign are cognitively dissonant when it comes to Britain's financial future – still insisting that the rest of the world will want us to trade with them and welcome us with open arms. People in this country need and deserve better from those in charge, not a playground spat in Eton's manicured grounds.

REMAIN

LOSS

The thing I will miss most is the freedom
for people to work and live wherever they
want to in Europe. I have a 10-year-old
son who has friends from some EU countries
whom he wouldn't have met otherwise.

What we might gain from not being in the EU
is a more difficult subject. I see less and less
positives in being an insular nation and narrowing
opportunities for our young people.

GAIN

Anton Dorson

	Royal Air Force flight sargeant
	55
born	Mauritius
educated	training at RAF Swinderby, Hereford,
	Halton and Cranwell
living	Northwood, Middlesex
working	retired

text received   25 March 2019

I am the son of first-generation immigrants and served for 38 years in the Royal Air Force.

Having lived in mainland Europe, I consider the right to controlled Freedom of Movement to be paramount. I also support and am thankful for the partnerships and organisations established to increase the security of the UK and Europe as a whole. My vote to remain was based on these considerations – and my fear that Brexit could lead to the wider fragmentation of the EU, endangering the North Atlantic Treaty Organisation that has provided such security for the EU and the world at large.

REMAIN

Since the referendum, events and political views emanating from the United States in particular, and from other more authoritarian powers, have hardened my belief we should remain in the EU and work to strengthen it.

Global collaboration.

We can't agree on everything, but being part
of the EU gives us more influence than we will
find in isolation. We are choosing to turn our
backs on a union that has international standing,
rather than modernise it from within. The
prospect of being outside the EU brings great
uncertainty – and all this because the majority

who voted feel disaffected because of the failings
of UK governments since 1972 and their inability
to bring about change. The EU should have been
challenged on some points of policy and the
UK could perhaps have righted these perceived
wrongs, but didn't. The UK helped the status quo
prevail, while many of its citizens felt subjugated
by EU policies.

Stronger border control might reduce under-the-radar people-trafficking and modern slavery. The lives of many young people, especially women, are destroyed by the actions of individuals who have a complete disregard for the law and human life. These are the people who should be the target of stronger border security, not the genuinely desperate individuals who flee many forms of persecution just so that they can survive. Tighter border control could also control the increase in the use of firearms in the UK.

GAIN

Dewayne Ector

music industry executive

40

born Trinidad

educated LLB (Hons) Law,
University of London

living London

working London

text received 25 January 2019

I am a proud Remain voter. Being in the EU provides the UK with so many more freedoms and options than leaving. The continuation of Freedom of Movement for both goods and people can only be a good thing. It provides trade opportunities for all and helps us integrate and become closer to our neighbours, which helps promote peace, understanding and acceptance of one another. In addition, the UK has done quite well within the EU by negotiating a favourable position. We have retained control of our borders by not joining the Schengen area. We have kept the pound and thus a high degree of fiscal independence. We make the most of the various grants and benefits that EU members have access to. It seems to me that the UK probably already has the best deal of all EU members by having one foot in and the other out. It seems quite stupid to give it all up.

REMAIN

LOSS

We will lose Freedom of Movement and thus
the option to easily live in another country that
might be sunnier!

We will have more autonomy and power over
our judicial system rather than relying on the   GAIN
European Court of Justice as the highest court.

Polly Ernest

chef, bed-and-breakfast owner
54

born Woking, Surrey
educated BA Clothing Marketing,
London College of Fashion;
NVQ Level 2 Professional Cookery,
Hereford and Ludlow College
living Hereford
working Hereford

text received 10 February 2019

I am one of the team behind the daily Stop Brexit protest outside Parliament. The protest started with one man in September 2017. He has been there every day that Parliament is sitting. I protest regularly with him and help administer and promote the protest. I am the founder of the grassroots group Herefordshire for EU.

I fundamentally believe that life is better when we share and forge bonds of friendship. I'm a big fan of not going to war as well. So I voted Remain without a moment's hesitation, for a peace project that had ensured the longest period of stability between previously warring nations. I believe that a supranational organisation not bound by the electoral cycle is a good thing and has afforded us much protection of our rights – from workers' rights, women's rights, environmental protection to health and safety. I welcome the influx of non-British EU citizens, who have massively contributed to our society both financially and culturally. 'Mieux ensemble' – better together, united in diversity.

REMAIN

LOSS

My children's birthright – Freedom of
Movement. I cannot understand why anyone
would choose to lose their right to live, love,
study, work and be treated without prejudice,
with equal access to healthcare, education
and welfare, in the 27 countries of the EU.

After years of political apathy, the strongest pro-EU movement in Europe is in the UK. Before the referendum membership of the European Movement was as low as 1,000 people. Now there are active branches across the country and in all major cities and towns.

GAIN

Jean Geldart

architectural assistant,
local government employee
71

born London
educated Architecture, Edinburgh University;
Postgraduate Diploma,
Labour Studies,
North London University

living London
working retired

text received 27 March 2019

I started work as an architectural assistant, but got involved in trade-union activity and ended up as a trade-union branch secretary for Unison. I've lived in London all my life and love its buzz, variety and inclusiveness. But I'm angry at the way its social fabric is being destroyed by government policies favouring the finance industry and big property developers, so young people can't afford to live here, and the people who make London a great place are being driven out. Those same policies have destroyed good industrial jobs all over the country, undermining local economies and creating the sense of exclusion that I think provoked many Leave voters. EU rules largely prevent the re-ordering of our economy, so I've always opposed our membership – but I couldn't bear to vote alongside the people making Leave an anti-immigrant crusade, so I did, in the end, vote Remain.

REMAIN

LOSS

The way the country has been divided. Intolerance and hatred have been stirred up, with each camp making caricatures of each other, and racism and xenophobia legitimised and encouraged by so many of the pro-Brexit politicians and media.

There was an upsurge in grassroots activism in reaction to the negativism of the referendum campaigns. It would be wonderful if the government shambles over Brexit persuaded millions of ordinary people that they must engage in politics, to 'take back control' in a real sense.

GAIN

Ioan Gwynedd

supermarket manager
33

born   Bangor, North Wales
educated   Diploma Travel and Tourism,
Brighton University
living   Caernarfon, North Wales
working   Bangor, North Wales

text received   09 March 2019

I am a shift manager at Lidl UK and live in Caernarfon, North Wales.

Why did I vote Remain? Because I am European. I was born and raised in Wales, which makes me British, of course, but my family are German. I feel more European than British. The EU is a fantastic concept that has brought so many positives to Wales, particularly via funding and grants – we have a massive agricultural industry, for example, which EU funding has helped immensely. The EU also provides grants to support both developing and developed businesses in rural communities. Brexiteers aren't looking at the wider picture. Not all of us live in thriving cities. I don't believe 'our' politicians will follow through and deliver the goods. They're shit – and have been for 20 years.

REMAIN

Just one?!

The breakdown of our relationship with mainland Europe, as obvious as it sounds. We're isolating ourselves and damaging our options, by inadvertently closing trade routes. The majority of Northern Ireland and Scotland voted Remain, but this was overlooked due to the voting system. As the overall majority in the UK voted Leave, the opinions of the different nations were overshadowed. Scotland might want independence from the UK now. I don't know how realistic this is, but it proves that Brexit isn't just fucking up our ties with the EU, it's also fucking up our relationships with each other.

LOSS

Absolutely nothing. I don't trust the government –
they're not capable of doing things properly,
as proven, ironically, by Brexit negotiations.
It has become a pissing contest, and they do not
have the best interests of the nation at heart.
It's devastating.

GAIN

Keith Jarrett

poet, writer, performer, educator
35

born London
educated BA Spanish,
University College London;
MA Creative Writing, Birkbeck,
University of London;
MA Writing in Education,
Goldsmiths, University of London;
PhD Creative Writing/
Study of Religion,
Birkbeck/SOAS,
University of London
living London
working London

text received 23 March 2019

I write poetry and fiction, exploring Caribbean history, religion, sexuality and Black British experiences. I am an international poetry slam champion, and was selected by Val McDermid as one of ten outstanding LGBT writers in the UK for the 2019 International Literary Showcase.

My play, *Safest Spot in Town,* was commissioned for the BBC's *Queers* series, and my poetry book, *Selah*, was published in 2017. I am a PhD scholar at Birkbeck, University of London, where I am completing my first novel.

I voted Remain for multiple reasons.
Here are some:

REMAIN

- I have friends and colleagues who will be adversely affected; I would never vote to make their lives more difficult!

- I thought the process would involve too many complications and unintended consequences to even consider any positives.

- Frequently running projects in Spain, and working at a UK university, I feared leaving would affect being able to apply for European grants and opportunities.

- I was repulsed by the dog-whistle racism that some people (not all but, undeniably, some) used in the campaigns.

- I believe Britain's membership in the EU helps build partnership and reciprocity.

- Blah blah blaaaaaaah! Who's listening, anyway?

I believe the biggest loss since the referendum is trust in each other.

I thought I might write something else: our sense of neighbourliness, our relative political stability over the last few decades, our standing as a financial stronghold, our right to easily live, work or just visit 27 other countries, or for our friends and loved ones to stay here, or something along those lines… but all of that relies on trust, to some extent.

Many people still see the UK and its people as stable and trustworthy, despite its ruthless history when dealing with the rest of the world. And on the whole, people living here trust the country and its systems, despite their shortcomings. All that has started to erode; we've started to burn bridges, using the fuel the politicians provided.

If I scratch my brains for something more positive, one unintended consequence has been a shift in the traditional divide between left and right, and even between classes. Given the fundamental divisions within parties, more people seem to agree the two-party system isn't working; political binaries are inadequate because life is more complex. If only we could translate this into more cross-party alliances, coalitions and, perhaps, proportional representation, we might enhance our democracy.

GAIN

Madeleina Kay

activist
24

born	Leicester
educated	BA Landscape Architecture, University of Sheffield, unfinished
living	Sheffield
working	Europe-wide
text received	08 February 2019

I was a student at the University of Sheffield when I voted Remain. My parents are both university academics, and I was brought up with an international outlook. I understood the opportunities and cultural experiences the EU provides to students and young people, and the importance of Freedom of Movement and research funding for UK universities. When the Brexit vote happened, it changed my life – I became an activist overnight. I decided to leave my course and adopt the identity of 'EU Supergirl', using art, music and writing to campaign against Brexit and, importantly, to promote the positive benefits of EU membership. Since the vote, I have self-published five illustrated fiction books about political issues and an information booklet, *24 Reasons to Remain*. I've also written and recorded protest songs, which I have performed at events across the UK and the EU. I passionately believe that we need to reform UK politics and work to make the political debate more engaging, informative and motivating, to empower citizens to participate in democracy. In 2018 I was awarded Young European of the Year for my work as an activist.

REMAIN

LOSS

The greatest initial loss to the UK is
the damage to our reputation on the world
stage. I am ashamed by the state of the
media, the nature of the political debate
in our country and the way our pathetic
excuse of a government has handled the
withdrawal process. We have become
a laughing stock in the eyes of the global
community. But the worst impacts of Brexit
have yet to come. I honestly believe the
most patriotic thing any British person can
do right now is to fight to save their country
by stopping Brexit.

The only 'Brexit Dividend' I can identify in two and half years of campaigning is the mobilisation of a huge community of pro-EU activists across the UK. If Brexit goes ahead, this community will be ready to lead the campaign to rejoin. It has been a privilege to meet and work alongside so many passionate individuals. We have also sent a message to the rest of Europe that many people in the UK still treasure our shared European values and believe in the dream of unity in diversity, and solidarity across nations.

GAIN

Matt Kelly

journalist
49

born Liverpool
educated A-level English,
Hugh Baird Technical College, Bootle
living London
working Norwich

text received 15 February 2019

After three decades in journalism, a period
of almost relentless decline in print sales,
launching a new national newspaper would
have seemed fantastical to me on 23 June 2016.
But on 24 June I woke up to a Britain split down
the centre between two new constituencies:
the 48 per cent and the 52 per cent. The Leave
voters seemed very well represented in national
newspapers, but not so much the Remain camp.
So I decided to launch a new weekly newspaper,
the *New European*, to fight their corner. We gave
ourselves a four-week life expectancy. Nearly
three years and more than 170 issues later, we
are still going strong. ¡Viva print!

REMAIN

LOSS   The luxury of political complacency.

A sense of perspective. Having to think hard about precisely why something you took for granted is so precious is a worthwhile exercise, even if you only do so when you're just about to lose it.

GAIN

Deborah Licorish

solicitor, judge
54
born Luton
educated BA English,
St Catherine's College, Oxford;
LLM Law,
Northumbria University
living Bradford
working Leeds

text received 13 January 2019

My parents were part of the Windrush generation. After university I worked in book publishing, before studying law and eventually qualifying as a solicitor. I have since practised as an employment lawyer. My master's degree dissertation looked at the limitations of discrimination law in the UK in the early 2000s. I currently sit as a part-time employment judge and am an accredited mediator. I am particularly interested in a collaborative, empathetic, 'interests-based' approach to resolving conflict at work – instead of both sides in a dispute spending most of their energy dwelling on the past and defending their adopted position, I help them to find a solution that is in their best interests. Through my work, I also appreciate how the EU has enriched labour laws in the UK.

I voted Remain.

REMAIN

LOSS

Since the 2016 vote, we have lost the art of respectful disagreement. Highly complex issues were grafted on to a simple question. Many will have voted thoughtfully; others, instinctively. Research shows that when we make decisions, we tend to adopt a position and thereafter justify it and argue about it. Few of us are prepared either to admit that our original decision may have been wrong in any way, or to refine or change our thinking. As a result, we become increasingly dismissive of anything that undermines or challenges our original position. And those who shout the loudest are usually on the shakiest ground.

As a result of the 2016 vote, however,
we have been presented with a golden
opportunity to follow a different but positive
path. Those who had been operating with
a sense of entitlement have been shaken to
the core. Others who were most comfortable
complaining from the sidelines have been
forced to step up to the plate. The journey
is going to be unpleasant and bumpy,
but, as William Blake identified, 'Without
contraries is no progression.' Those with
sufficient empathy and vision will be able
to hear above the din, and harness the
positive passion and energy to bring about
much-needed change. I see this starting to
happen now on a personal and social level –
for example, through the use of peer-to-peer
mediation in schools. I am still waiting to
see who will provide the political leadership
we so desperately need.

John Moffatt SJ

priest, teacher
60

born Romford, Essex
educated MA Classics,
Christ Church, Oxford University;
MTh (Theology),
University of Innsbruck

living London
working London

text received 22 January 2019

I'm a Jesuit Catholic priest and teacher.
I studied Classics and Philosophy at university.
Since joining the Jesuits in 1982, I've taught
at their two comprehensive schools in London,
and worked as a university chaplain and in
adult education. I'm currently a student again in
London. I've lived in Austria, Germany and South
Africa, and holidayed in France, Spain, Italy and
Greece. For reasons of culture, education and
personal connection, I feel myself to be British,
English and European. And Ancient Greek.

When it came to the vote, I felt that, for all
its faults, compromises, subterfuges and
ethical blind spots – and, as with any political
organisation, they are many – the EU project
was both a noble effort to do something good
together and a platform that gave us Brits
a stronger international voice than our size
strictly merited. To me, the country during the
2000s had become a more prosperous, more
open place than the fractious, anxious island
that I remembered from the 1970s and early
1980s. I liked being British this way, collaborating
on a common project with our neighbours,
bringing our own skills and insights to the table,
building relations of respect, prospering through
our collaboration, sharing in a commitment to
democracy and human rights.

REMAIN

So here is my chosen loss – one possible future, a bit lugubrious:

The vote to leave was not just about cancelling our subscription to an organisation that no longer serves our purposes. We have sent the world a message about who we are and how we want to be in the world: a small, self-assured nation (fine), fortified against the outside world (highly ambivalent), flexing its economic muscles in free-for-all, bring-it-on competition (caveat emptor). This is at a time when the economic forces that control the global agenda are shifting power in new directions, and when solidarity among those who claim a commitment to the rule of law, social justice and human rights is threatening to dissolve. We have chosen national pride and shark-infested waters. The sharks and the wealthy among us will do fine (they always do), and where reality falls short of rhetoric, the more jingoistic demagogues will just find someone else to blame (they always do). Meanwhile, the rest of us may find not just that we have to pay a price, but that the price includes our soul.

Here is my chosen gain – another possible future, a bit dreamy:

The shock of the vote has already shaken political alignments and imaginations within the UK. Let's suppose (as many sensible people seem to do) there are further shocks to come, not just to the UK, but to other nations within and beyond continental Europe (even prominent Leave campaigners grant there will be no easy ride into their future). Perhaps these shocks will spur new forms of political and economic organisation, less driven by a warped idolatry of transactional economic efficiency, less destructive of local communities and the planet. Perhaps those twentieth-century structures, which were a response to that century's global crises (and largely shaped by the historical *idées fixes* of Europeans and the US), are now crumbling before new realities. And if we are playing a part in that disintegration, perhaps we will also play a part in the creation of a new, sustainable order that preserves the best insights of our European heritage and does justice to the many voices and cultures of the world.

Charlie Mullins
OBE

businessman
66

born	London
educated	plumbing apprenticeship, London
living	London
working	London

text received 01 March 2019

I am the archetypal entrepreneur! My beginnings were humble – I grew up on a south London estate – but I went on to start Pimlico Plumbers, building it from scratch into a £50 million enterprise, despite leaving school with no qualifications. I did complete a four-year apprenticeship, though, and am a staunch advocate of apprenticeships as a result.

I played a very vocal role in the anti-Brexit movement, to begin with as part of the Remain campaign, and more recently in the fight to stop the UK leaving the EU. I have said from the very beginning that Brexit makes no sense – all it does is slam the door in the face of half a billion potential customers, leaving the UK with the task of coaxing them to let us back in again.

REMAIN

LOSS

The repercussions of the referendum campaign, and its result, have driven a wedge through communities and regions of the UK, to the point where the country may never feel properly like one nation ever again. In a hundred years, 2016 may be the moment historians credit with the beginning of the breakup of the UK.

We have learned that our system of representative democracy is a far more efficient and less divisive system of government for dealing with complicated issues than more direct methods of democracy such as referendums.

GAIN

Colin Murphy

comedian
50

born County Down, Northern Ireland
educated Art and Design Foundation,
Bristol Polytechnic;
BA Design,
Belfast School of Art,
Ulster University
living Belfast
working UK; Republic of Ireland

text received 12 March 2019

I was born in County Down, Northern Ireland and now live in Belfast, working as a stand-up comedian.

I voted Remain because the argument for leaving was nonsensical. I perform all over the UK and throughout Ireland; my agent is Dublin-based; my wife's family lives in Dublin; my children regularly play sport in Dublin; one of my son's university choices is in Dublin – so any future changes to border arrangements between the UK and Ireland will have a direct effect on how we live our lives.

REMAIN

LOSS

Trust in cold hard facts and the opinions of people who actually know what they're talking about seems to have been replaced by emotion, patriotism, sentimentality and an enormous sense of innate superiority.

Westminster knows Northern Ireland exists.
Though the politicians, and the media and
the British public, still don't actually care
about us, or our history, or the border,
or even the difference between the United
Kingdom and Great Britain. To misquote
Oscar Wilde, 'There is only one thing in the
world worse than being talked about, and
that is being talked at.'

Or:

GAIN

We now know for absolute definite
that a crowd of completely and utterly
ill-informed, incompetent, self-serving
bastards govern the UK.

Or:

It's easier than ever to start a fight with
a stranger.

Or:

Knowing that you didn't vote for this shambles.

Femi Oluwole

co-founder and
chief spokesperson,
Our Future Our Choice
29

born Darlington
educated BA Law with French,
University of Nottingham
living Birmingham
working UK-wide

text received 19 January 2019

I was born in Darlington, lived in Swansea, went to school in Dundee and grew up in Bromsgrove. I studied Law with French and began a career in European human rights, working in Brussels and Vienna. I cut short my dream traineeship to come back to the UK and stop Brexit. I have been using my knowledge of EU law to inform the debate since 2016.

As co-founder and chief spokesperson of Our Future, Our Choice, a youth campaign for a People's Vote, I tour the country to promote discussion of the issues that underlie the referendum decision. I make videos and appearances that focus on the facts about Brexit and the EU that are often ignored by politicians, and these have been seen by millions across the UK.

REMAIN

Instead of fixing divisions in society, the referendum has cemented them by creating a binary opposition between Leave and Remain. The underlying issues that led people to vote Leave have not been addressed by the government's deal: people voted for more sovereignty, more money for our NHS, and more control over immigration. The deal accomplishes none of these things: it would leave us bound by EU rules with no say over them, with an NHS significantly worse off (according to the British Medical Association), and without the EU citizens who make up 5 per cent of our population but 10 per cent of our doctors.

Brexit has managed to shine a light on the
anger and frustration of people who, as
a result of regional inequalities, have been left
behind by years of government neglect and
underfunding. It has also motivated people
to get involved in politics so that Brexit doesn't
ruin everything – young people in particular
are overwhelmingly pro-EU. They are making
their voices heard, campaigning against
the prospect of decades of instability and
reduction of rights.

GAIN

Sol Papadopoulos

film and television producer
and director
58

born London
educated BSc Marine Engineering,
University of Liverpool;
16mm intensive course
National Film School, London
living Liverpool
working Liverpool

text received 15 January 2019

My love for a good tale has taken me into factual and fictional storytelling for both film and television. Recent feature documentaries include biopics on the life of Jack Jones, the Liverpool-born trade unionist and International Brigade fighter, and the poet Emily Dickinson. I have produced three feature films with Terence Davies – 'Britain's greatest living film director' – and *Sometimes Always Never*, starring Bill Nighy, which premiered at the London Film Festival 2018.

I'm a rabid Remainer. I consider myself more European than British. I was born and bred in London but have lived most of my adult life in a maverick city that voted to remain: Liverpool. I was attracted to the city partly because of the spirit of its people, who consider themselves more Celtic than English. There's even an anthem at Liverpool FC that declares, 'We're not English, we are Scouse!' Identity has always interested me. Born of immigrant parents from two ends of Europe – Cyprus for my father and the west of Eire for my mother – I identify as European. For a long time I've wanted an Irish passport but never got one until now. I'm contemplating opening a Dublin office for my film company, Hurricane Films, and have joined the Screen Producers Association in Ireland.

REMAIN

The loss for me is that the UK as a whole will be perceived as anti-European, even those who didn't vote to leave.

Producing feature films is an international business that requires the co-operation of financiers, distributors, producers and sales agents. It's a minor miracle whenever a film comes together: it takes like-minded people working across borders and cultures, trusting each other and sharing the ideals of the project. It's a joy when it comes off, but it is never without challenges. Now, whenever I deal with colleagues in Europe, I have to preface every meeting with an apology for the state of our nation.

LOSS

For me, leaving has no gain. I don't believe we will leave, but I will try to enter into the spirit of the question. The last two and a half years have shown us to be a divided nation. Bizarrely, I'm going to cite this as my gain. Those that represent us have been woken from their complacency as never before. How the UK is governed needs serious rethinking – it needs to go beyond the bubble of Westminster and to be far less metrocentric. Whatever the final outcome of Brexit, we have the opportunity to shake this up. Now.

Fran Piddlesden

	marketing manager
	32
born	Dover, Kent
educated	BA, MA English Literature,
	University of Warwick;
	CIM professional diploma
	in Marketing
living	Canada, previously London
working	Canada, previously London

text received 15 January 2019

I voted Remain; it didn't occur to me to vote to leave. I grew up in a time when evidence of a peaceful, uniting EU was everywhere – in language-learning at school, the freedom of cheap travel, discovering new foods, the mix of friends at university, the perspectives of films and books. The possibility of escape to another country was always present – exchanges, holidays, semesters abroad – the harmonious comings-and-goings of people. This is beyond the practical realities of the distribution of food, medicines, labour, all of which I took for granted.

I don't want to be part of a Britain that appears too arrogant to see the benefits and stability of working collectively. I have taken myself, and my savings, from London to Canada.

REMAIN

LOSS   We've lost our external, collaborative outlook.

We have the chance to reset our consumerist behaviour and rebuild our economy in a more environmentally sustainable way.

GAIN

Jo Quinton-Tulloch

	museum director
	52
born	Ilford, Essex
educated	BSc (Hons) Biological Science, University of East Anglia; MSc Science Communication, Imperial College of Science, Technology & Medicine
living	Bradford
working	Bradford
text received	18 January 2019

I voted to remain because the world
faces unprecedented challenges – climate
change, population growth, pollution,
wars, civil unrest and increasing xenophobia.
I believe that to tackle these challenges,
we need to share responsibility and work
collaboratively to create a better future. This
requires us to build alliances, develop shared
understanding and collective ownership,
to value differences and recognise the power
of working together. It is nonsense to think
that we would be better off as individuals
or as a society if we work in isolation.
The world is too small and interconnected –
we require global collaboration to create
a sustainable future. Remaining in the EU
supports a collaborative ethos and provides
a mechanism to enable action.

REMAIN

LOSS   The ability of UK citizens to live, love and
        work freely in Europe.

An increase in the number of young people who have an active interest in the political process.   GAIN

Simon Richardson

108–111

	engineer
	58
born	London
educated	MA, Engineering Science,
	Magdalen College, Oxford University
living	Aberdeen, Scotland
working	retired

text received 05 March 2019

I was born in London but have lived in
Scotland for most of my adult life. I am married
and have two grown-up children. I have just
retired from a 35-year career as an engineer
in the oil industry, latterly leading a team
developing the Clair field – the largest in Europe
and one of the most technically challenging.
I have a lifelong passion for climbing and
mountaineering that has taken me all over
the world. I am now as likely to be tying onto
a rope with someone from a different country
as with someone from the nation of my birth.

REMAIN

I voted Remain because I believe we can
have a stronger influence on our continent as
a member of the EU than outside it. The EU
is by no means perfect, but we can promote
change more effectively from within.

LOSS

The UK's influence (and the contribution of its citizens) will be diminished. I have learned that great things can be done when people with diverse backgrounds and nationalities work together constructively. This applies to complex engineering projects as well as climbing difficult mountains.

The overhaul of the UK's political system.
I would like to see a formal constitution,
greater clarity on the decision-making powers
of government and Parliament, and high-quality
individuals with wide life experience entering
politics. I feel unrepresented by any political
party at present.

Toby Roberts

	civil engineer
	61
born	Malaysia
educated	BSc, PhD, Civil Engineering,
	Kings College London
living	London
working	Hertfordshire

| text received | 20 January 2019 |

I am an entrepreneur, geotechnical expert and director of a civil-engineering company working in the UK, Ireland, Europe, the Middle East and Canada. I was born in Malaysia; my mother grew up in India and my father was a British Army officer. I was brought up variously in Canada, Hampshire, Singapore, Berkshire, Yorkshire, Gloucestershire, Germany and Kent. My wife is half Norwegian.

I voted Remain because I like Europe. I love the architecture, landscape, food, wine, people, the weather and the sea. I recognise that the EU is not really about any of this but I would like my children to have the same opportunity to travel freely, to work in Europe and to feel welcome. I also believe that close cultural, intellectual and economic ties to our nearest neighbours enrich all involved. In a world of large trading blocks and vast corporations, where many of the vital challenges we face require transnational cooperation and agreements, being part of the EU gives us a much bigger voice. Whilst the EU certainly has flaws, these can only be tackled from the inside.

REMAIN

LOSS   **The nation has lost its mind!**

The referendum mobilised people who felt disengaged from politics, who blamed the injustices and inequalities of life in Britain on bureaucrats in Brussels rather than on our elected representatives in Westminster. It was their engagement that gave Leave its 'winner takes all' 4 per cent majority.

It should be a good thing that more people are voting, but, as Churchill observed, 'No one pretends that democracy is perfect or all-wise. Indeed, it has been said that democracy is the worst form of government except all those other forms that have been tried from time to time.' Perhaps this divisive referendum will shock Parliament into updating our political system so that our elected representatives take the whole nation's views into account, recognising that we all seek a better future for our planet, our country, our communities, our families and ourselves.

GAIN

Rachel Stephen

NHS Human Resources staff
47
born Trinidad
educated Bachelor of Business Administration,
Andrews University,
Berrien Springs, Michigan;
MA Leadership and Management,
University of Greenwich;
MA Human Resource Management,
University of Hertfordshire
living Laindon, Essex
working Basildon, Essex

text received 27 January 2019

I am originally from Trinidad and Tobago. I migrated to the UK with my French husband in 2000 and am currently employed in the NHS. We chose this country because of its diversity and the opportunities it offered my family. School exchange programmes have given my sons the chance to travel to France, Germany and Spain, to make new friends and explore new countries. It was a very sad day on 24 June 2016 when their school informed them that the UK would no longer be part of the EU and explained the implications this might have.

REMAIN

My vote in the referendum was to remain. I knew the Leave campaign's claims of financial benefits for the NHS were just to attract votes. The area where I live voted to leave, but many of the people who voted were elderly. I think they felt too many foreigners were taking advantage. Despite this vote, in 2019 the local MP voted against the deal drafted by Theresa May.

LOSS

Our children have learned unity and togetherness through the EU, now they are part of a bitter divorce.

Leave supporters are happy. GAIN

Simon Weller

	trades union general secretary
	51
born	Oakham, Rutland,
	moved as baby to Cyprus
educated	O levels,
	Steyning Grammar School,
	West Sussex
living	Brighton
working	UK-wide
text received	13 March 2019

I was raised in a number of places including Lincolnshire, Sussex and Norfolk, moving about because my father was RAF aircrew. I joined British Rail as a teenager, as a driver's assistant, and began train driving at 21. I was a train driver for 20 years, before being elected Assistant General Secretary of ASLEF (the UK train drivers' union). I am also a member of the TUC's General Council.

I voted Remain. The EU is flawed in its pursuit of privatisation, but I still prefer it to the option of a hard-right Conservative Party with its vision for working people and further deregulation. The notion of 'Lexit' – a left-wing Brexit – is attractive, but it's self-indulgent to contemplate: it is not on offer. All the Tories want to do is create an environment that makes them richer. Crisis capitalism.

REMAIN

There is no such thing as a 'jobs-first Brexit'. The change in the global economy over three decades has fundamentally redefined manufacturing. Leaving the customs union means just-in-time manufacturing will become unworkable. This will destroy jobs and will be the UK's death knell as a powerful world economy.

Leaving the EU would allow a left-leaning government to rescind the 2016 EU Fourth Railway Package, designed to create a Single European Railway Area. It mandated the division of the railway infrastructure from railway operations, the privatisation of services, and opened domestic rail markets to private operators.

GAIN

Donna Williams

university course director
54

born Llanelli, South Wales
educated Visual Communication,
North East Wales Institute;
MA Counselling Practice,
University of Wales,
Trinity Saint David
living Llanelli, Carmarthenshire
working Swansea, South Wales

text received 25 February 2019

I am a senior lecturer at an art school,
a counsellor and a mum. I have travelled and
worked around the world, but settled back
where I began in Llanelli, an industrial,
hard, wonderful, kind town with salt-of-the-
earth people.

I voted Remain. Wales has been greatly
supported by the EU. I don't think everyone
understood this, or the impact of leaving.
I happened to be in Greece when the result
came in. It was during the European Football
Championship, and I went from feeling
pride to feeling despair that my country
had voted out. Many of my friends working
in local factories are now losing their jobs.
All of them refused to engage in this book.

REMAIN

So many friends and family voted Leave.
It's something we don't talk about, but it has
created division and hatred in my community.
Even though I voted Remain, when the result
came in, I felt that I had let down my ancestors –
the men and women from my family who fought
and died in wars so that one day we would
be together in peace. There is nothing more
powerful and more frightening than a nation
divided. It is only the people of power, who
create division, that truly benefit.

LOSS

I lost a partial sense of belonging. I was
extremely shocked by the fact that in
my hometown 56.7 per cent voted Leave.
I felt disappointed, sad and disconnected
from neighbours near and far.

I have had to wake up. Finding myself completely out of touch with my local community, friends and family, meant that something needed to change. I have been on a mission to try to understand. I am still trying. I think many who voted Leave now regret it, but it's time to accept and be creative in how we move forward.

GAIN

Rebecca Willis

environment and sustainability
researcher
47
born Cyprus
educated BSc Social and Political Sciences,
King's College, Cambridge University;
PhD Lancaster University
living Cumbria
working Lancaster

text received 07 February 2019

I am a researcher with 20 years' experience in environment and sustainability policy and practice, at international, national and local level. I am a research fellow for the IGov project at the University of Exeter, investigating energy governance. With Lancaster University, I am conducting research into political responses to climate change. I advise the Lake District National Park, where I helped to establish the UK's first local carbon budget; I have a particular interest in local and distributed energy solutions. I was a member of the Natural Environment Research Council, and I am an associate of the think tank Green Alliance – I founded their Climate Leadership Programme, an initiative to support members of the UK Parliament. I have worked as a policy adviser at the European Parliament in Brussels, specialising in international environmental issues.

I voted Remain because I believe the UK is stronger as part of a group of like-minded countries.

REMAIN

LOSS

Working together to protect the natural world and combat climate breakdown. The EU has been a force for good on the environment and we will struggle without them.

The howls of protest, both for and against Brexit, highlight that we have become very bad at engaging people in the political process. This might be the moment that we realise we can't tackle the huge environmental and social challenges we face unless we work with people, take account of their views, and build a more grown-up politics.

GAIN

Denise Wilson

	teacher, psychotherapist
	72
born	Sunderland
educated	BEd English and Drama, Northumbria University; MA Counselling Psychology, Durham University; Dip Humanistic Counselling and Psychotherapy, Stockton Institute of Counselling and Psychotherapy
living	Sunderland
working	retired
text received	08 February 2019

I was born in Sunderland in a one-bedroom, no-bathroom, toilet-at-the-bottom-of-the-yard flat to working-class parents. I went to the local grammar school, then took a teaching degree, followed by a master's. I have taught English and Drama at a comprehensive and worked as Head of Student Services, then Deputy Director, in further education, before becoming a psychotherapist in private practice.

I voted Remain for much the same reason I voted for us to stay in the European Community in the first referendum in 1975 – to someone born at the end of the Second World War, there seemed a greater chance of peace if countries were linked in this way. In 2016, though the EU was far from perfect, I liked the idea of a multicultural world. I noticed EU regeneration money was distributed more fairly than national funds too. I have never been nationalistic. My identity – English from Irish ancestry – leans more to workers of the world. This focus perhaps sounds idealistic, perhaps unrealistic, but I believe that we should seek justice and acceptance for all people from all corners of the world. Here in this country we have much to learn as well as share.

REMAIN

A rather shaky innocence.

The referendum dispelled any cosy idea that we are largely a tolerant and homogeneous society. We have been confronted by the issue of difference. I was and am a Remainer, and was greatly surprised by friends and acquaintances who voted Leave. Initially, I asked myself whether I knew these people as well as I thought; I struggled to feel empathy for them. Yet, on reflection, I had no problem understanding the Leave vote in this north-east working-class area that has always struggled to secure decent resources for living. Sick of Conservatives whose policies, communication and background showed an indifference to our ever-worsening condition, voters in the 'forgotten' north exercised the small amount of power that was given. Now people see that big companies like Nissan have no great loyalty to the region. It is predicted this area will be the hardest hit by leaving. We were lied to by all. My heart breaks for the people here.

A shaky solidarity.

There are few economic or social positives
for the north-east. The differences between
north and south are evident in the inequality
of resources of all kinds, including justice.
We are learning to bear these differences and
are united in disgust at a chaotic and largely
self-promoting political system. For some,
the powerlessness is paralysing. But we will
do what we have always done: hunker down,
help each other, fight on, issue by issue,
group by community group, largely ignoring
the political parties – including Labour –
who have let us down. We have been brutally
reminded that help comes mainly from within.
We are outraged and march and shout for
change. Let the media work on the side of
the poor and the oppressed for once! It will
be chaotic but survivable.

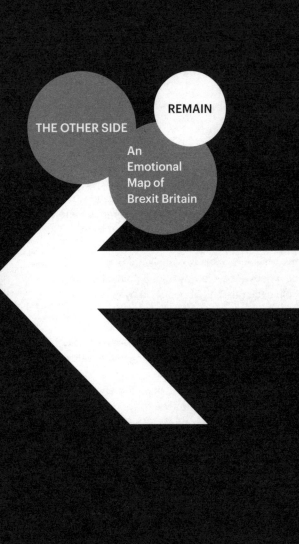

REMAIN

THE OTHER SIDE

An
Emotional
Map of
Brexit Britain

LEAVE

THE OTHER SIDE

An
Emotional
Map of
Brexit Britain

I believed by leaving the EU we would gain increased spending on the NHS, more jobs for UK workers, and would take back control of immigration and our borders. Freedom of Movement has led to an increase in NHS tourists. I have looked after several patients who clearly stated that they only came to the UK for treatment. A lot are non-English-speaking and the cost of interpreters has to come out of our hospital budgets. Hopefully leaving will ease the NHS overspend.

GAIN

LOSS

I believe the loss to the UK will be a shortage of foreign skilled workers, doctors, nurses and specialists.

I've been a senior healthcare assistant in a NHS hospital for the past 16 years, where I have noticed vast changes, not all of them good. This is one of the reasons I voted Leave.

LEAVE

Michelle Stokes

156–159

	healthcare assistant
	58
born	Sittingbourne, Kent
educated	NVQ Level 3
	Health and Social Care,
	Maidstone Hospital
living	Kent
working	Kent
text received	13 January 2019

What I hoped to gain from voting Leave
was the flexibility and agility to be innovative
and pioneering in the world. I trust that our
government will make the right decisions
to ensure that we progress with what's right
for all people, our economy and the planet.

GAIN

LOSS

What I'm sad to lose is being an active member of Europe, which has such a rich and diverse heritage and culture – I'm still a European and proud of it. I love the fact that London is so multicultural and enjoy hearing from international friends how they love our country.

I have over 20 years business experience working as a manager in large multinational organisations, and have lived and worked in Asia and the Middle East as well as the UK. As a management consultant I have worked on large, international change-management programmes. I have developed European business strategy and managed global projects, leading and collaborating with teams across many different cultures. I now run my own executive coaching company.

I voted Leave because I feel that the EU is not fit for purpose organisationally and not willing to reform for the 21st century. I'm also sad that no member of the EU came to campaign and make the emotional case for the UK to stay part of the union.

LEAVE

Maia Rushby

executive coach
48

born Blackburn
educated BSc Chemistry,
York University
living Richmond, Surrey
working London

text received 19 March 2019

The referendum has resulted in greater engagement in political and philosophical debate – what is the UK's place in the world, how much does the EU do for us, what policies can address society's ailments?

As citizens become more engaged, hopefully more meaningful legislation will be passed. We can hold our public officials to greater scrutiny, not just in terms of Brexit, but in all matters of state. Those previously unrepresented now have a greater voice – the poor, young and minorities. All those whose lives will be most affected by Brexit are suddenly being heard louder than before. That change is irreversible and Brexit was the catalyst. Let us hope it leads to greater and better things.

GAIN

Division.

The referendum has heightened division and instead of healing with time, it's been exacerbated. Brexit is at the forefront of national conversation, which means the urgency to tackle other pressing problems is lost. Public faith in our leaders has reached a nadir as they agonise to reach consensus and implement Brexit. The executive enjoys no support from the legislature – it is held in contempt and viewed as untrustworthy by the international community. The House of Commons is paralysed by one question: Leave or Remain? It will take a generation to recover from this division.

LOSS

I was born and raised in east London, then studied Maths and Economics, interning in the financial services industry. After graduating, I developed medical technology applications for six months before becoming an associate in a multinational venture-capital firm. I've been privileged to meet its dynamic founders across the world, people creating fantastic new inventions in the UK. Brexit will impact heavily on my industry and the UK's global reputation.

I voted Leave, but have since switched emphatically to Remain. I was erroneously enticed by the possibility of a global Britain, striking free-trade deals with every wealthy nation possible, free of the 'shackles' of Eurocrats determined to stymie British progress at every opportunity. Instead of doing research, I trusted officials who I assumed were knowledgeable. I never considered the benefits of the Customs Union, the Single Market or the complexities of the Irish border question. I was wrong. I believe Brexit will determine the UK's destiny for the rest of this century. Continued membership of the EU represents Britain's greatest hope of prosperity for its people, for Europe and for the world.

LEAVE

Division.

The referendum has heightened division
and instead of healing with time, it's been
exacerbated. Brexit is at the forefront of national
conversation, which means the urgency to tackle
other pressing problems is lost. Public faith in
our leaders has reached a nadir as they agonise
to reach consensus and implement Brexit.
The executive enjoys no support from the
legislature – it is held in contempt and viewed
as untrustworthy by the international community.
The House of Commons is paralysed by
one question: Leave or Remain? It will take
a generation to recover from this division.

LOSS

I was born and raised in east London, then studied Maths and Economics, interning in the financial services industry. After graduating, I developed medical technology applications for six months before becoming an associate in a multinational venture-capital firm. I've been privileged to meet its dynamic founders across the world, people creating fantastic new inventions in the UK. Brexit will impact heavily on my industry and the UK's global reputation.

I voted Leave, but have since switched emphatically to Remain. I was erroneously enticed by the possibility of a global Britain, striking free-trade deals with every wealthy nation possible, free of the 'shackles' of Eurocrats determined to stymie British progress at every opportunity. Instead of doing research, I trusted officials who I assumed were knowledgeable. I never considered the benefits of the Customs Union, the Single Market or the complexities of the Irish border question. I was wrong. I believe Brexit will determine the UK's destiny for the rest of this century. Continued membership of the EU represents Britain's greatest hope of prosperity for its people, for Europe and for the world.

LEAVE

LEAVE

THE OTHER SIDE

An
Emotional
Map of
Brexit Britain

I believed by leaving the EU we would gain increased spending on the NHS, more jobs for UK workers, and would take back control of immigration and our borders. Freedom of Movement has led to an increase in NHS tourists. I have looked after several patients who clearly stated that they only came to the UK for treatment. A lot are non-English-speaking and the cost of interpreters has to come out of our hospital budgets. Hopefully leaving will ease the NHS overspend.

GAIN

LOSS

I believe the loss to the UK will be a shortage of foreign skilled workers, doctors, nurses and specialists.

I've been a senior healthcare assistant in
a NHS hospital for the past 16 years, where
I have noticed vast changes, not all of them
good. This is one of the reasons I voted Leave.

LEAVE

Michelle Stokes

	healthcare assistant
	58
born	Sittingbourne, Kent
educated	NVQ Level 3
	Health and Social Care,
	Maidstone Hospital
living	Kent
working	Kent
text received	13 January 2019

What I hoped to gain from voting Leave
was the flexibility and agility to be innovative
and pioneering in the world. I trust that our
government will make the right decisions
to ensure that we progress with what's right
for all people, our economy and the planet.

GAIN

LOSS

What I'm sad to lose is being an active member of Europe, which has such a rich and diverse heritage and culture – I'm still a European and proud of it. I love the fact that London is so multicultural and enjoy hearing from international friends how they love our country.

I have over 20 years business experience
working as a manager in large multinational
organisations, and have lived and worked
in Asia and the Middle East as well as the UK.
As a management consultant I have worked
on large, international change-management
programmes. I have developed European
business strategy and managed global projects,
leading and collaborating with teams across
many different cultures. I now run my own
executive coaching company.

I voted Leave because I feel that the EU is not
fit for purpose organisationally and not willing
to reform for the 21st century. I'm also sad
that no member of the EU came to campaign
and make the emotional case for the UK to
stay part of the union.

LEAVE

Maia Rushby

	executive coach
	48
born	Blackburn
educated	BSc Chemistry, York University
living	Richmond, Surrey
working	London

152–155

text received 19 March 2019

The referendum has resulted in greater engagement in political and philosophical debate – what is the UK's place in the world, how much does the EU do for us, what policies can address society's ailments?

As citizens become more engaged, hopefully more meaningful legislation will be passed. We can hold our public officials to greater scrutiny, not just in terms of Brexit, but in all matters of state. Those previously unrepresented now have a greater voice – the poor, young and minorities. All those whose lives will be most affected by Brexit are suddenly being heard louder than before. That change is irreversible and Brexit was the catalyst. Let us hope it leads to greater and better things.

Simranjeet Riyat

venture-capital associate
23
born London
educated BSc/MSc
148–151 Mathematics and Economics,
University of Surrey
living London
working London

text received 11 February 2019

Terra incognita.

GAIN

LOSS   **Status quo.**

I am a former Director of Architecture, Design and Fashion at the British Council and former editor of *Blueprint* magazine. I'm currently working for Lantao Design Academy to set up a study programme to enable collaboration between Chinese and European designers, and I'm curator of an exhibition about Samuel Beckett for London Festival of Architecture. I am an internationalist who has always opposed immigration controls, and this is partly why I voted Leave.

To me, Europe and European culture is not dependent on what I see as an undemocratic technocracy, but is about the genuine links we have with our neighbours. The EU has turned Europe into a fortress to keep 'non-EU' people away. I hope that leaving will lay the basis for a new type of international solidarity, where Europe is porous to the rest of the world and where national governments can be held to account by the public. Since the referendum, politics has opened up in a very exciting way. For the first time in years there is the possibility for change. It feels as if we're living through history – and even making it!

LEAVE

Vicky Richardson

architecture writer and curator
50

born London

educated Art Foundation,
Central School of Art and Design;
BA Architecture,
University of Westminster;
MA Early Modern History,
King's College London

living London
working London

text received 21 January 2019

An opportunity.

The opportunity to take back control of
UK borders, to ensure that we can continue
to benefit from an excellent NHS, outstanding
education system and superb housing. We
have a responsibility to protect the services
that others worked so hard to create.

GAIN

LOSS

An idea.

The idea of a group of countries joining together as one, united by similar goals and aspirations, with the intention of supporting and assisting each other to achieve these aims. The theory being that we are more powerful when we are united.

I have lived in Birmingham all my life, leaving school at 16 to become a policewoman. I left the force to marry, starting a family when I was 25. I was a full-time mum of three until I was 40 and then trained as a reflexologist, working from home for 18 years. I am now retired and enjoying my grandson. As a grandmother, I am concerned for the children of our country.

I voted Leave because we are constantly bombarded with worrying news – there is not enough housing, there are too many children in our schools and not enough teachers, our NHS is in crisis, without enough doctors. The reasons services have declined are, of course, complicated. But it is clear that there are too many people living in the UK and the infrastructure to support them is not in place. Our island needs to control the numbers of people arriving from all over the world every day. Without an infrastructure to support people, it is ludicrous to do nothing. EU citizens, I'm sure, make up only a fraction of the new people living in the UK, but we have to begin to control our borders. The EU gave us no support with this problem.

LEAVE

As newly elected Leader of the Opposition, Conservative MP Margaret Thatcher supported the 1975 Yes campaign, on the grounds of free trade. However, as prime minister from 1979, she argued for small government and deregulation, becoming increasingly opposed to further European integration, as she made clear in her famous 1988 Bruges speech to the College of Europe: 'We have not successfully rolled back the frontiers of the state in Britain only to see them reimposed at a European level with a European super-state exercising a new dominance from Brussels [home of major EEC institutions].'

The British media's position on Europe
changed radically during the 1980s,
shifting from 'quiet or just plain uninterested
acquiescence in the European project...
to a vigorously partisan hostility bordering on
a nationalist and in some arenas xenophobic
approach'.[4] Negative and often exaggerated
EU stories have continued to increase in
number and vitriol ever since, particularly
in the popular and right-leaning British press.
Writing for the *Daily Telegraph* in his role
as Brussels correspondent from 1989 to 1994,
Boris Johnson mainstreamed the negative
portrayal of EU affairs. His biographer,
Sonia Purnell, credits him with making
Euroscepticism 'an attractive and emotionally
resonant cause for the [political] Right'.[4]

The Daily Telegraph

MONDAY, SEPTEMBER 21, 1992

French say Yes to Maastricht

Razor-thin majority for treaty leaves future of unity moves in doubt

OUI 51.6%
NON 48.8%

Lamont hints at interest rate cut

Major is given more room for manoeuvre

Pound falls against the mark and franc

Sweden failed for straying into Iraq

Airline

The EU was established via the Maastricht Treaty of 1992. This treaty aimed to facilitate 'ever closer union' and a shared currency between member states. In opposition to Maastricht, Eurosceptic parties took root in the UK. The Referendum Party was active from 1994 to 1997, while the Anti-Federalist League, established in 1991, was renamed the UK Independence Party (UKIP) in 1993.

Sun
1 November 1990

Owned by Australian-born American media mogul Rupert Murdoch, the *Sun* heaped scorn on the call by Jacques Delors, EC president, for a European Central Bank and single currency.

Daily Telegraph
21 September 1992

In the French referendum to ratify the Maastricht Treaty just 51 per cent voted Yes. In the UK parliamentary sovereignty allowed the Conservative government to ratify it without a referendum

2016 EU Referendum
Three Leave Campaigns

In 2006 Nigel Farage became UKIP leader, campaigning on a platform that included immigration controls. In the 2014 European elections UKIP made gains, often from the Conservatives. Under pressure from Eurosceptics in his own party, Prime Minister David Cameron included in the 2015 general election manifesto a commitment to hold a public referendum on EU membership if the Conservatives achieved a majority. They unexpectedly did so.

There were multiple Leave campaigns in the 2016 referendum. Vote Leave (the official campaign), UKIP and Leave.EU all played on people's fears about immigration. Targeted Vote Leave Facebook adverts employed maps and infographics that falsely claimed Turkey was joining the EU and immigration from the region was imminent. Leave.EU Twitter posts included images of Islamic terrorists to incite similar fears. UKIP's 'Breaking Point: The EU has failed us all' poster showed a long line of refugees crossing the Croatia-Slovenia border. It was criticised by Leave and Remain campaigners alike; Twitter users drew attention to its similarity with Nazi propagandist footage.[5]

BREAKING POINT
08450 752 752
BREAK POINT
The EU has failed us all
We must break free of the EU a
08450 752 752

UKIP

UKIP Breaking Point poster
2016

Showing a queue of mostly
non-white people crossing
the Croatia-Slovenia border
during the refugee crisis
of 2015, the campaign
poster (preceding page, top)
was reported to the police
for potentially breaching
UK race laws.

UKIP supporter
2013

Despite the UK opting out
of the Euro when it ratified
the Maastricht Treaty,
UKIP's branding continues
to use the pound sign
logo (preceding page,
bottom) as a mark
of British independence.

In 2019 the House of Commons Digital, Culture,
Media and Sport Committee published its
final report on an 18-month investigation into
disinformation and fake news.[6] This included
scrutiny of campaign materials in the EU
referendum. The committee concluded that
'Democracy is at risk from the relentless
targeting of citizens with disinformation',[7]
and that electoral law was 'not fit for purpose'.

Leave.EU Twitter post
2016

Designed to incite fear,
the Twitter image (top
right), now deleted, was
condemned for implying
a link between terrorism
and EU membership.

Leave.EU Twitter post
2016

Boris Johnson campaigned
with Vote Leave. However,
Leave.EU referenced
him (right) slamming the
government's 'Project Fear'
(the Remain campaign's
focus on the risks of
leaving the EU).

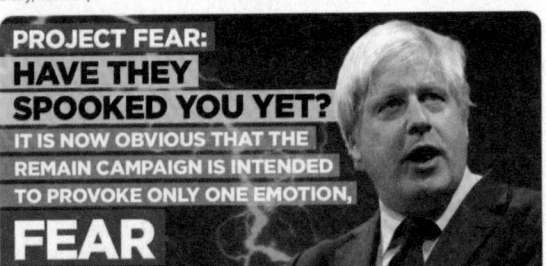

There were a number of allegations regarding unlawful campaigning during the EU referendum and in 2018 the Electoral Commission, an independent body that regulates party and election finance, found that Vote Leave's spending 'broke the electoral rules set out by Parliament to ensure fairness, confidence and legitimacy' and fined it £61,000.[8]

Vote Leave bus
2016
A key tool of the campaign, the bright red bus was emblazoned with bold white lettering and carried the familiar NHS logo to support its claim that leaving the EU would release funds for healthcare.

Vote Leave website messaging
2016
While appearing to impart facts, the official Vote Leave campaign site employed bite-sized text, infographics and provocative imagery that sometimes misled.

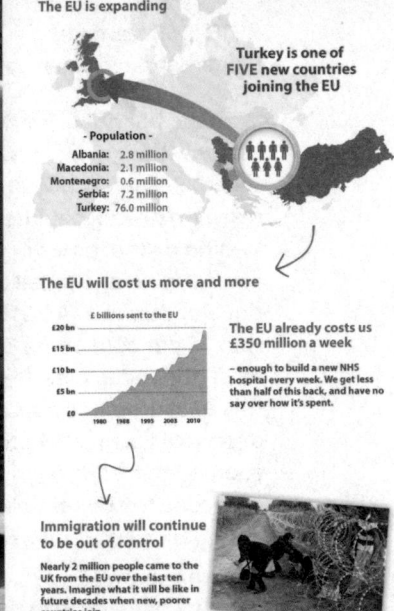

The EU is expanding

Turkey is one of FIVE new countries joining the EU

- Population -
Albania: 2.8 million
Macedonia: 2.1 million
Montenegro: 0.6 million
Serbia: 7.2 million
Turkey: 76.0 million

The EU will cost us more and more

£ billions sent to the EU

£20 bn

£15 bn

£10 bn

£5 bn

£0

1980   1988   1995   2003   2010

The EU already costs us £350 million a week

– enough to build a new NHS hospital every week. We get less than half of this back, and have no say over how it's spent.

Immigration will continue to be out of control

Nearly 2 million people came to the UK from the EU over the last ten years. Imagine what it will be like in future decades when new, poorer countries join.

Vote Leave's slogan 'Take Back Control' resonated across the UK political spectrum, as did the message emblazoned across its campaign bus. While the £350 million figure was attributed to poor research,[9] anger at the 'cost of EU membership' became the third most cited reason for supporting Leave in the weeks before the vote.[3] The NHS, having suffered cuts under government austerity programmes, inadvertently became a Vote Leave campaign tool in one of the most memorable images of the referendum campaigns.

2016 EU Referendum
Government Remain campaign

With the benefit of hindsight, it is easy to see why the government's Remain campaign failed. Research indicates that there is a growing divide 'between those who feel left behind by the forces of globalization and mass immigration and those who welcome such developments'.[3] A 2016 YouGov poll showed that 72 per cent of the British public didn't trust 'the ruling elite'.[9] Considered against this backdrop, the confident Remain identity, despite its clear evocation of the UK flag, seemed to be speaking only to the people who reap the benefit of open markets, liberal economics and increased immigration.

A government 16-page A5 leaflet went to every household in the country. A mix of simple text, data and large images, it employed a visual language associated with authoritative, neutral information design. While being professional and confident, it appeared top-down and, most importantly, emotionally detached. It didn't speak to those who felt left behind, to the people for whom voting Leave was often an expression of 'frustration, rage, resentment, and insult – as well as hope that a vanishing way of life could be saved and a proud national identity celebrated'.[10]

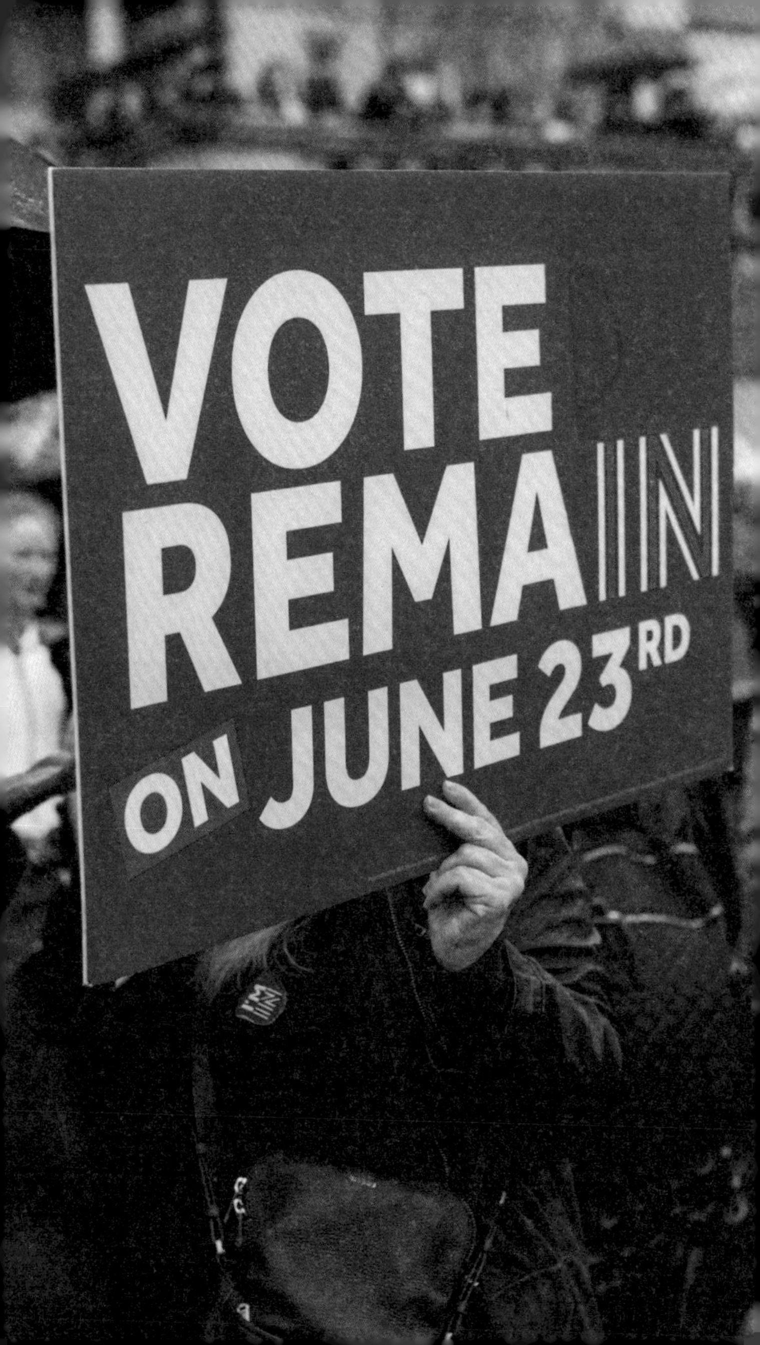
VOTE
REMAIN
ON JUNE 23RD

Britain Stronger
in Europe Campaign
2016

Designed by branding
experts North, the official
Remain campaign identity
(preceding page) played
on the word IN and
referenced the UK flag.
It was accomplished,
but failed to connect
emotionally with voters.

Government leaflet
2016

All UK households received
this government leaflet
(right, bottom and overleaf)
setting out the case
for Remain. The design
is visually neutral but
was off-putting to all but
genuinely engaged readers.

A stronger economy

The EU is by far the UK's
biggest trading partner.
EU countries buy 44% of
everything we sell abroad, from
cars to insurance. Remaining
inside the EU guarantees our
full access to its Single Market.
By contrast, leaving creates
uncertainty and risk.

The EU's Single Market has
over 500 million customers
and an economy over five
times bigger than the UK's.
The Single Market makes it
easier and cheaper for UK
companies to sell their
products outside the UK,
creating jobs as a result.

Being inside the EU also
makes it more attractive
for companies to invest in
the UK, meaning more jobs.
Over the last decade, foreign
companies have invested
£540 billion in the UK,
equivalent to £148 million
every day.

UK industry and the EU

Industry	Jobs	Share of exports going to EU
Aerospace	110,000	47%
Chemicals and pharmaceuticals	136,000	54%
Financial services	1,069,000	41%
Food manufacturing	373,000	53%
IT and telecoms	1,364,000	46%
Transport	1,065,000	44%

Why the Government believes that voting to remain in the European Union is the best decision for the UK.

The EU referendum, Thursday, 23rd June 2016.

ESSAY

Over 3 million UK jobs are linked to exports to the EU

Improving our lives

Cost of living

If the UK voted to leave the EU, the resulting economic shock would put pressure on the value of the pound, which would risk higher prices of some household goods and damage living standards.

Losing our full access to the EU's Single Market would make exporting to Europe harder and increase costs.

Travel abroad

Millions of UK citizens travel to Europe each year. The EU has made this easier and cheaper.

EU reforms in the 1990s have resulted in a drop in fares of over 40% for lower cost flights.

From next year, mobile phone roaming charges will be abolished across the EU, saving UK customers up to 38p per minute on calls.

EU membership also gives UK citizens travelling in other European countries the right to access free or cheaper public healthcare.

Some argue little would change if we left the EU. But there are no guarantees UK customers would keep these benefits if we left.

Controlling immigration and securing our borders

Securing our borders

The UK is not part of the EU's border-free zone – we control our own borders which gives us the right to check everyone, including EU nationals, arriving from continental Europe.

Immigration

The Government has negotiated a deal that will make our benefits system less of a draw for EU citizens. In future, new EU migrants will not have full access to certain benefits until they have worked here for up to four years. The Government will have greater powers to take action where there is abuse of our immigration system.

Some argue that leaving the EU would give us more freedom to limit immigration. But in return for the economic benefits of access to the EU's Single Market, non-EU countries – such as Norway – have had to accept the right of all EU citizens to live and work in their country.

Keeping us safer

EU membership means UK police can use law enforcement intelligence from 27 EU countries, and will have access to fingerprint and DNA information.

EU cooperation makes it easier to keep criminals and terrorists out of the UK. Since 2004, using the European Arrest Warrant, over 1,000 suspects have faced justice in UK courts and over 7,000 have been extradited.

If the UK voted to leave the EU, the resulting economic shock would risk higher prices of some household goods

The UK is not part of the European border-free zone. We control our own borders

040–041

At 72.21 per cent, the turnout of registered voters for the 2016 referendum was high, but the margins were narrow. Leave won with 51.89 per cent of the vote, leaving the UK bitterly divided – often on grounds of personal identity. Both of the UK's main political parties pledged to stand by this outcome, although the nature of the future relationship with the EU was still to be determined.

As the government negotiated with the EU, and sought approval of its Brexit deal in Parliament, Remain-supporting individuals and independent groups employed ingenuity and visual wit to argue for a second vote or to draw attention to the potentially negative outcomes of leaving the EU with or without a deal.

The Mayor of London, Sadiq Khan, endorsed
overt messaging during the 2017 New Year's
Eve fireworks, when the London Eye was lit up
to resemble the EU flag, and eyebrows were
raised when the queen opened Parliament
in 2017 sporting a blue hat circled with yellow
flowers. The queen's dresser has since said
this was pure coincidence.

London Evening Standard
21 June 2017

At the State Opening
of Parliament, the hat
worn by the politically
impartial queen left
people wondering what
it signified.

London's New Year's Eve
fireworks
31 December 2017

Designed to emphasise
the 'London is open'
theme, the firework display
clearly referenced the
EU flag.

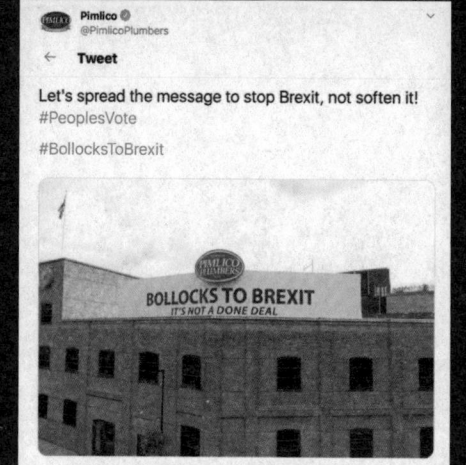

Pimlico ✓
@PimlicoPlumbers

← **Tweet**

Let's spread the message to stop Brexit, not soften it!
#PeoplesVote

#BollocksToBrexit

BOLLOCKS TO BREXIT
IT'S NOT A DONE DEAL

4:17 pm · 27 Sep 2018 · Twitter Web Client

1.5K Retweets **4K** Likes

Businessman Charlie Mullins adorned his company HQ with a 41-metre 'Bollocks to Brexit' sign. Stickers spoofing Royal Mail failed-delivery cards spread via Twitter after the original Brexit date was postponed. And four friends formed Led by Donkeys, a guerilla billboard action group that evolved into legal, crowd-funded advertising campaigns to highlight pro-Leave politicians' broken promises and changing positions.

Signs and spoofs
2018–19

'Bollocks to Brexit' sign overlooking the tracks into London's Waterloo station and 'Sorry, we tried to deliver your Brexit' spoof Royal Mail card.

Sorry, we tried to deliver your Brexit

Time	Today's date 29 / 3 / 19
Number	

You were lied to and your:
- [ ] Unicorn
- [x] Country
- [x] Brexit
- [ ] Empire
- [x] Good Old Days before all the foreigners came

could not be delivered to you

because
- [x] It doesn't exist
- [ ] It was stolen from you by Remoaners
- [x] Turns out they don't need us more than we need them

Please see over the rainbow for where your item is now

*Please bring a valid form of ID like maybe, oh I don't know, a blue passport, with you to collect your item

#bsads   blackscore

David Davis ✔
@DavidDavisMP

If a democracy cannot change its mind,
it ceases to be a democracy.

9 Nov 2012

He didn't tweet it, he actually said it!
In a speech 'Europe: it's time to decide'. What changed?

#LedByDonkeys @ByDonkeys

044–045

"WE DIDN'T VOTE TO LEAVE

WITHOUT A DEAL"

MICHAEL GOVE

Led by Donkeys
Billboards, signs,
projections
2018–19

Whether projected on
England's Europe-facing
cliffs, unfurled at protests
in Parliament Square,
incised into sand and
visible from space,
or pasted on billboards,
Led by Donkeys' anti-Brexit
stunts have used visual
wit and inventiveness.

ESSAY

The original date set for the UK to leave the EU was 29 March 2019. This was renegotiated to 31 October 2019 when Parliament couldn't agree to ratify the deal proposed by Prime Minister Theresa May. A parliamentary majority did, however, agree to oppose a no-deal scenario.

The necessary extension to EU membership meant that the UK had to take part in the 2019 EU elections. The poor showings for Conservative and Labour in those elections were testament to the frustration of the UK electorate. Leave supporters felt let down that the UK had not yet left, while Remain voters were angry that neither party represented their views.

Two parties were the beneficiaries – the
Liberal Democrats and the new single-issue
Brexit Party led by Nigel Farage (the former
UKIP leader). The Brexit Party branding was
controversial. Employing a fresh turquoise
colour, it included an arrow resembling
a house on its side that was also similar to
the directional arrows used outside every
polling station.

**Liberal Democrat materials
2019**

'Bollocks to Brexit' was used
on T-shirts and stickers by
Remain supporters before
becoming the official slogan
of the pro-Remain Liberal
Democrats in the 2019 EU
elections.

**Guido Fawkes tweet
9 May 2019**

As tweeted by pro-Leave
website Guido Fawkes,
a professor of psychology
complained to the Electoral
Commission that the Brexit
Party arrow points to the
voting box on ballot papers.

048–049

Theresa May failed to persuade MPs
to support her EU withdrawal deal and
the ensuing Conservative leadership contest,
decided by party members, delivered the
expected successor. Vote Leave campaigner
Boris Johnson became prime minister
on 23 July 2019. Conservatives hoped
he would deliver Brexit quickly, reducing
Brexit Party support.

'Get Ready for Brexit'
Government campaign
2019

Created by the agency
Engine, the campaign
reinforced Johnson's
core message to 'get
Brexit done'.

'Get Ready for Brexit' spoof
2019

Opponents were quick
to send up the government
campaign, subverting
its simple type-only design,
ironically set in DIN, the
font used for German
road signage.

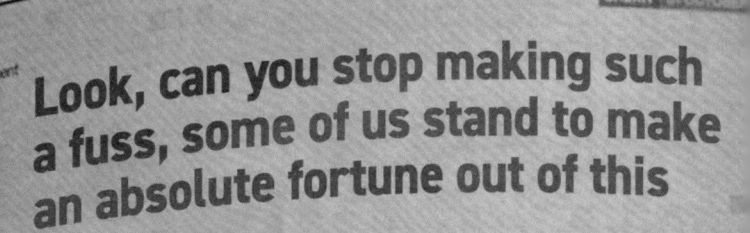

Look, can you stop making such a fuss, some of us stand to make an absolute fortune out of this

>> Prepare for Brexit at gov.uk/brexit

Boris Johnson's tactics were controversial. They included threatening to leave without a deal if one wasn't agreed in time (despite the consequences outlined in the government's Yellowhammer report),[11] unlawfully suspending Parliament, and withdrawing the whip from Conservative MPs who voted against him. Meanwhile, the government's 'Get Ready for Brexit' campaign launched in September 2019, placing the onus on individuals and businesses to prepare via an online checker, which immediately prompted multiple visual spoofs. The UK did not leave the EU on 31 October 2019 and a general election was called.

2019
General election and beyond

Surprisingly, UK political advertising is not regulated by the Advertising Standards Authority. The non-partisan Coalition for Reform in Political Advertising described this as a 'fake news and disinformation general election'.[12]

'Get Brexit Done' was theConservative electoral campaign mantra. Emblazoned on billboards, buses and backdrops, and repeated incessantly, the slogan was clear, concise and memorable. University of Surrey politics professor Simon Usherwood noted that it also tapped into a 'sense of frustration that... this is dragging on and on'.[13] The Conservative victory was achieved in part through success in Leave-voting constituencies where this message persuaded voters to switch political allegiance.

The Conservatives' official campaign was accompanied by less transparent materials. A leaflet re-appropriating NHS branding was criticised as misleading, with one Twitter user commenting that they only realised it was a Conservative party leaflet because the phrase 'get Brexit done' featured in the text.

As this book goes to press it looks likely that the UK will leave the EU on 31 January 2020.

'Get Brexit Done'
Conservative campaign
2019

According to Benedict Pringle in *Campaign*, this 'action-oriented' slogan was 'one of the greats of recent electoral history'.[14] Focus groups 'revealed [it] was the only slogan that undecided voters could remember'.

A prescription for
a stronger NHS
Conservative campaign
2019

Conservative sub-campaigns were eclectic in design. Shown here is a controversial example that on first glance could have been mistaken for a bona fide NHS leaflet.

ESSAY

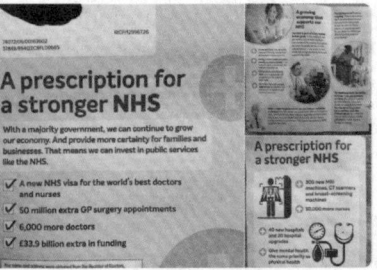

Paul Waugh ✓
@paulwaugh

Follow ∨

So here's the latest Conservative leaflet in a
Con/Lib marginal.
Made to look like an NHS prescription.
Doesn't mention word Conservative or Boris
Johnson anywhere in the copy (apart from v
small print).
But says vote for "a majority govt".

A prescription for
a stronger NHS

With a majority government, we can continue to grow
our economy. And provide more certainty for families and
businesses. That means we can invest in public services
like the NHS.

✓ A new NHS visa for the world's best doctors
   and nurses
✓ 50 million extra GP surgery appointments
✓ 6,000 more doctors
✓ £33.9 billion extra in funding

A prescription for
a stronger NHS

5:56 am - 7 Dec 2019

About the typefaces
Paul McNeil

This book uses 14 different sans serif typefaces, all designed since 1945, as a form of code. The UK map opposite shows the 12 electoral regions returning MEPs in EU elections. Each region has been assigned a typeface, which is used for the texts of contributors living in that area. As the fonts were allocated to regions alphabetically, no association between their characteristics and the regions is implied. One contributor was in mainland Europe at the time of the vote, signified by another typeface – and also in the set is Graphik, the house style for GraphicDesign&.

In the wake of the Second World War many Europeans sought a sense of order, justice and neutrality, ideas that influenced contemporary design practice. Informed by modernist social ideals, an initiative from Switzerland became one of the most influential design movements of the twentieth century. Called the International Style, it emphasised clarity, organisation and objectivity, resulting in several new sans serif typefaces in which extraneous elements were deliberately eliminated. Two of the best known are Univers and Helvetica, but many of the 14 fonts used in this book share these characteristics.

For more about the history and characteristics of each typeface flip the book over and turn to pages 024–037.

Scotland
Haas Unica

North East
Folio

Northern Ireland
FS Koopman

Yorkshire & Humberside
Univers

East Midlands
Akkurat

Eastern
Aktiv Grotesk

North West
Forma

Wales
Rail Alphabet

London
Arial

South West
Neutral

South East
Helvetica

West Midlands
Replica

Mainland Europe
Untitled Sans

Throughout
Graphik

Glossary

Serif
Small strokes added to the ends of letterforms in serif typefaces.

Sans serif
Typefaces that do not have serifs.

x-height
The height of a lower case 'x'.

Grotesque
Style of sans serif from the nineteenth and very early twentieth centuries. Less monoline and geometric than those that came after. Sometimes referred to as Gothic.

Terminal
Any stroke which does not terminate in a serif.

Leading
The distance between baselines, also called line-spacing.

Counter
A fully or part-enclosed space within a letter.

We asked 26 Leavers to tell us a little of their life story, why they voted the way they did, and to cite one loss and one gain they could imagine following the 2016 result.

LEAVE

Richard Aherne

	sheep farmer
	56
born	Snowdonia
educated	Glynllifon Agricultural College
living	Snowdonia
working	Snowdonia
text received	20 February 2019

I am a Welsh sheep farmer in the mountains of Snowdonia. After studying at the local agricultural college, I spent a year working in America and New Zealand before taking over a 70-acre farm at the age of 19 and building it up to the 1,100-acre farm it is now. From a business perspective, I should have voted Remain in order to safeguard the Common Agricultural Policy. However, I voted Leave. I have become sick of the gradual absorption of Britain into an enlarging super-state of Europe that allows our politicians to make pre-election promises which, when they fail, can be blamed on the EU. As a voter within Europe, I felt my voice getting fainter and fainter.

LEAVE

LOSS

The divisions thrown up by this issue are,
I'm afraid, going to lead to a fractured nation
pulling itself apart, while the rest of Europe
and the world look on in bemusement.

I hope that over the next decade we will come together as a nation with pride and a renewed identity, trading on the world stage. I also hope that the British public will seek out British produce and products when making their purchases.

GAIN

Michael Arrastia

software developer
49

born London
educated BSc Computer Science,
Bristol University
living Bristol
working Bath

text received 11 March 2019

I have a Spanish background so many
are surprised that I voted Leave. Over
decades I have followed fairly dispassionate
reporting in the Spanish press of EU affairs.
I have seen relations that are fractious,
self-interested and dominated by a handful
of powerful, overbearing nations. Countries in
the Euro-zone have their budgets scrutinised
by the European Commission to ensure
they comply with a long-standing policy
of austerity. European funds for regional
development have failed to improve the
south's impoverished labour market and,
when things have gone badly, as in Greece,
there has been a brutal lack of solidarity.
The EU has a privatisation and market-led
economic agenda that has failed millions
of working-class Europeans. Politically,
the EU is an institution with legislative
and executive structures that are top-down,
obscure, bureaucratic and undemocratic.
The mantra over the years has been 'more
Europe' – whatever that means, it's not
something I adhere to.

LEAVE

LOSS

It's hard to tell at this stage. But personally, I will be shedding the uncomfortable feeling of being part of an organisation I do not believe in.

An opportunity, albeit slim, to take Britain
on a different course – away from centralised
politics and the prevailing EU doctrine of
free-market economics.

Gordon Bridger

development economist
91

born Argentina
educated BSc Economics,
London School of Economics;
MA Economics,
Manchester University
living Guildford, Surrey
working retired

text received 05 February 2019

I was born in Argentina, but at the age of 20 worked my passage to Liverpool, before settling in Manchester. I have worked with the United Nations and the British Ministry of Overseas Development, where I was Economics Director for Country Programmes. My career has taken me to most developing countries, and involved many meetings in Brussels when I was employed by the EU as a consultant. The lessons I learned through my work informed my Leave vote:

1 Immigrants provide energy and ideas, which spearhead change, but they need to integrate and not overwhelm countries.

2 The success of economic development is dependent on stability and social flexibility, and relies upon policies that allow individual enterprise to flourish. Aid can help if it supports local efforts. Setting spending targets for aid entails waste – around £5b per year could be saved with targeted, smaller, better-quality aid.

3 Institutions have as their main objective the interests of those who work for them. Monopolies, private or public, eventually inhibit growth. International organisations are under-staffed and recruitment is based on national quotas – all on huge salaries. EU bureaucracy is a serious inhibitor to development.

LEAVE

The unhappiness of Remainers.

The gain is economic.

Since 1998 the UK deficit with the EU has increased from £10b to nearly £100b. Despite this, since 1999 the British economy has grown by 42 per cent, faster than Germany, at 32 per cent. In 2018 *Forbes* magazine reported Britain as the 'number one country to do business in'. Conversely, the EU economy is not healthy. There is high unemployment, especially in Mediterranean countries, due to the Euro crisis. These countries have debts they cannot repay, and equally they cannot devalue. Their young people are leaving. Germany looks secure due to its huge exports, but half of these have not been paid for (largely by Italy), which accounts for 30 per cent of Germany's GDP.

We will be much more prosperous once we leave what has become a failing international bureaucratic institution.

Alex Brierley

	ground staff, Wimbledon
	27
born	Burnley, Lancashire
educated	National Diploma in
	Sportsturf Management,
	Myerscough College, Preston
living	London
working	London
text received	26 January 2019

I wasn't sure what I wanted to do after school but one summer I visited the Wimbledon Championships, where my brother worked as one of the ground staff. I met the guys and decided that this was where I wanted to work. I studied Sportsturf Management then moved to London, going to Wimbledon on seasonal contracts for the next six years. In 2015 I was lucky enough to become full time.

I voted Leave because I don't like the idea of laws that will affect us being passed in other countries. Our laws should be determined and set by the people we elect. I never understood how people in Brussels could set laws for 28 member states and expect them all to comply. Each country has different ways of living. I think people linked to terrorism have taken advantage of human-rights laws in recent years; the fact they can go to the EU court to overrule a British court is absurd.

I felt with the option to leave I had to try and make my vote count, and to change things, hopefully for the better.

LOSS   Increased travel cost to European countries.

More control over skilled and unskilled
worker immigration.

GAIN

Simon Clark

composer, organist, pianist
44
born Kent
educated Composition,
Royal Academy of Music;
BA Classics,
St Mary's University, Twickenham
living Suffolk
working Suffolk

text received 12 February 2019

I am a composer and freelance organist and tutor. People have been taken aback to hear that someone who is both highly educated and working in the creative arts voted Leave, as I did. In their eyes, my voting choice didn't match with my demographic. This, to me, sums up why it was a seriously bad idea to have a referendum in the first place. It has caused division in families, in communities and in society at large. There are constant generalisations made about the profile of the voters on either side – erroneous ones in many cases. I didn't want a referendum, but we got one. The thing that was uppermost in my mind was how people would look at Britain in the history books in a hundred years or more. Did we have the courage and self-confidence to strike out on our own and be a self-determining country once again? As things stand, we are still to discover whether this is true.

LEAVE

LOSS

It is possible, regardless of whether
we end up with a hard or a soft Brexit, that
we might lose influence in the world at
large. It occurs to me that this was inevitable
anyway, with the Empire long gone, so
I'm not sure this particularly worries me.

Determining our own laws, taking charge of our own money and taking back our borders – but this all depends on whether what we get is a true Brexit or just BRINO (Brexit in Name Only).

GAIN

Tim Cummins

engineering consultant
73

born Bradford, West Yorkshire
educated BA Psychology/Anthropology/
Economics;
MSc Business Administration,
Durham University
living Elton, Cambridgeshire
working Elton, Cambridgeshire

text received 13 January 2019

I have consultancy experience working in the UK, China, India, EU, US, Australia, Singapore and Scandinavia, mainly in engineering businesses.

I voted Leave. The EU's present structure is unsustainable, because its flaws are unaddressed. Currency union without political union is an impossibility. Unelected decision-making is anathema. Economic inequality between countries is fudged or ignored. Youth unemployment levels are frightening. Regulation is growing rampantly, helping Brussels to grow and flourish. Economic growth is negative, as are interest rates. There are now soldiers on borders to control immigration between EU countries. Populist factions are rising as citizens feel that Brussels is not relevant.

I believe the general UK population does not want to lose its British identity or be subject to control by an external political organisation. A sovereign UK has a long, confident and proud history of fighting to remain democratic and independent. I believe it can flourish internationally with direct control of its institutions and destiny.

All Remain arguments focus on fear of leaving – there has been no positive case made for staying.

The big loss is faith in the processes that have guided the UK's 'government by consent' system. There is now clear division between government and the majority who voted. When governments do not give proper regard to the expressed will of the people, democracies go wrong and unexpected people take charge, as in Brazil, France, Austria and even Germany. And, of course, in the USA, where Trump convinced those who were feeling let down by Washington that he would come to their rescue. We have seen energetic attempts to overturn and frustrate Brexit. These may well succeed. There will be trouble coming in the future.

The gain from the Brexit vote was that the people, in a record turnout, clearly expressed their confidence in the UK's capabilities as an independent nation, and their desire to regain sovereignty and control as a democratic and civilised country. This was not some kind of sinister nationalism or expansionary ambition. It was simply the wish to regain identity and make an independent future, instead of playing an increasingly subordinate role in an entity where the leadership is not chosen by the people and which is remote, unresponsive and occasionally hostile.

GAIN

Baroness
Ruth Deech, DBE

academic, lawyer,
bioethicist, politician
75

born London
educated MA Jurisprudence,
St Anne's College, Oxford University
living Oxford
working London

text received 16 February 2019

I attended Christ's Hospital in West Sussex, a boarding school that provided free education for children from modest backgrounds. On my ninth attempt, I was admitted to St Anne's College, Oxford, where I read Law. Later I was Law tutor at the college and then Principal from 1991. I chaired the Human Fertilisation & Embryology Authority from 1994 to 2002 and discovered a world of infertility, ethics and scientific advances. From 2004 I was the first Independent Adjudicator for Higher Education, handling student complaints at the national level; then regulated the Bar as chair of the Bar Standards Board. I was a governor of the BBC at the time of the disputed Iraq war 'sexed-up dossier'. I was appointed a crossbench peer in 2005 and speak about higher education, women's issues, disability, and to defend Israel.

I have been a Leaver for at least 25 years, because I attribute to the EU's lack of democracy and its drive to federalism the resurgence of extreme nationalism, antisemitism, and breaches of human rights across Europe. The Union is fracturing and failing and there is nothing the UK can do to restore it.

LEAVE

Dialogue that leads to understanding.

Obsessive Remainer friends cannot imagine anyone they know voting Leave. They can barely bring themselves to talk to me once they discover I am a Leaver. This is clear in the sneering about ignorance at the dinner tables of Hampstead and North Oxford – You are the only intelligent person I know who voted Leave, they say. There is now a deep schism in British politics – quite unlike and much deeper than the Labour-Tory differences – that will not heal for a generation, and defies explanation. I now have to probe gently to find out whether acquaintances are of the same persuasion, and if they are, we treat each other as if members of a secret society. The subject is banned from social gatherings, while I realise that the pro-EU sentiments of high-flying friends go no deeper than the Polish plumber and the cottage in France!

No longer being chained to events and developments in the EU that offend my belief in human rights and self-determination.

I will no longer feel shame sharing responsibility for the EU and its members' failures: discrimination against minorities; refusal to accept the EU quota of migrants; breaches of the rule of law; fences between states to keep migrants out; attacks on journalism and free speech; corruption in the judiciary; rising extremism, xenophobia and antisemitism; overdependence on Russian oil; the lack of a united moral European foreign policy; no intervention over Kosovo and Crimea, and the abuse of rights in Turkey; impoverishment of Greece; the Euro crisis; interference with governments and budgets; ignoring the results of referendums; lack of visible independence of the European Court of Justice; crushed Catalan self-determination; the split between the West and the Visegrád states still in the shadow of their former Soviet oppressors; German dominance and protectionism.

Julie Drain

residential childcare worker
66
born Accrington, Lancashire
educated Certificate of Qualification
in Social Work,
Accrington College of Further Education
living Clayton-le-Moors, Lancashire
working retired

text received 16 January 2019

As a 'Baby Boomer', I benefitted from government subsidies in housing and education and received a good level of income from the age of 16. Jobs were abundant, mortgages and retirement packages affordable. It saddens me that following generations are not as lucky – that poverty and food banks are currently a way of life for professional working families. The world has not improved with time.

I voted Leave. I expected our government to plan and execute a credible way forward and not the Brexit fiasco of the last two years. I believe that if our government put public interest first, and not party politics, our exit could be straightforward.

My vote was for change. Britain, predominantly the north, is decimated: industry, education, law and order and local authorities all need money injected to make them strong again. I would like the outrageous amount of money being spewed into the EU to be used for this purpose. Regarding immigration, if Britain governed its own borders, we could change the rules to admit people willing to work and earn but not expecting welfare. This would apply for Brits in Europe too, of course.

LEAVE

LOSS

The European Single Market that allows goods
and people to move around as if in one country.

Britain having more power and not being overruled.   GAIN

Tony Ellerbeck

	Royal Naval Officer, airline pilot
	75
born	Harrogate, Yorkshire
educated	Britannia Royal Naval College, Dartmouth;
	Royal Naval College, Greenwich
living	Somerset
working	retired
text received	19 January 2019

I was a Fleet Air Arm pilot, subsequently
commanding a ship before leaving
the Navy to become an airline pilot flying
from Heathrow. Post 9/11 I took on a
specialised role in aviation security. Later,
as a consultant, I wrote papers on the threat
of terrorism to aviation and also worked
on European Defence Agency projects.
In 2010, while working on an EDA project,
I had a close insight into the structure
of the EU and its strategy. We were told
that after 2021, UK foreign interests would
be handled by the European Commission
ambassadors, of whom there are currently
some 110 worldwide. Given that the EU has
a Commission, a Council, a Parliament, an
overriding Court of Justice, ambassadors,
a Central Bank, the Euro, a flag and an
anthem, I consider that the EU has morphed
into a de facto federal state. I don't wish
Britain to be a part of it, so I used my vote in
the promised 'once-in-a-lifetime referendum'
to vote Leave.

LEAVE

LOSS

Restriction to the service industries
working with businesses and consumers,
particularly the loss of passporting rights
for the financial sector.

Resumption of independent sovereignty.

Helena Fenn

mental-health support worker
38

born Derby
educated BA Philosophy and
Business Management,
University of Lampeter, Wales
living Birmingham
working Worcestershire

text received 05 March 2019

I work as a mental-health support worker
in the NHS. I voted Leave because I believed
that the UK government needed to be able
to make laws based on what was appropriate
for the UK. Some of this was about setting limits
on who could come into the country, but never
about evicting people who have studied, worked
and contributed to our society while we have
been in the EU. I wanted our government
to have more autonomy and accountability.

LOSS

Unity. There has always been an element
of division within the UK, but this has got
bigger and the UK has become more unstable.
Each country has a different view on Brexit
and what they want – and no one can agree.
We are divided by culture, religion and ethnicity;
divisions are fuelled by angry debates over
immigration and who has the right to live here.

More control over our own policies and
law-making, though this outcome seems
further away now than I'd hoped.

GAIN

Steve Forrest

	photographer
	57
born	Manchester
educated	BA Design for Communication/Advertising, Manchester Polytechnic; MFA Fine Art, Goldsmiths, University of London
living	Manchester
working	Manchester
text received	25 January 2019

After graduating I spent an unsatisfying three years as an art director in London ad agencies. Since 1992 I've been working as a photographer, first on a free local paper in Oxford, then six months living in the Gaza Strip, five years working for an agency in Bradford, one year living in Eritrea photographing the war against Ethiopia, and 10 years working as a freelance portrait photographer for the *New York Times* in London. I now work predominantly as a commercial photographer and have moved back to Manchester after 25 years living inside the London bubble.

There are many reasons why I voted Leave. I believe the upper echelons of the EU are undemocratic. I was appalled by the EU treatment of African and Middle Eastern refugees – and of Greece after their financial crisis. I don't support the foreign military adventures, in Libya and Syria, for example. I was distressed by the way the working-class were written about before the referendum; by the dismantling of our public services, in part informed by the EU's fixation on competition rather than quality of life; and finally by the austerity, led by the EU and US, which has seen millions thrown out of work worldwide.

The Left self-destructs.

I find the diminished respect for old people, working-class communities, and people left behind as the neo-liberal capitalist juggernaut races forward quite disgusting. My fear for the future is that right-wing parties will capitalise on the vacuum left by Labour.

Democracy is revitalised.

The biggest-ever mandate for change in the UK's history was delivered by the people – despite overwhelming business and political pressure to vote Remain. We now have a chance to develop our own future. We can increase training for the young and unemployed instead of relying on cheap foreign labour, renationalise the vital transport and energy sectors (illegal under current EU regulations), and finally make our own politicians more accountable to the people, instead of unelected and unaccountable EU bureaucrats.

GAIN

Lucy Harris

campaign director
28

born East Anglia
educated BMus Music,
City University, London;
MA Publishing,
University College, London
living London
working London

text received 19 February 2019

I am the director of Leavers of Britain, a social networking campaign to unite Leave voters across the country over a pint or a coffee. A passionate supporter of Brexit, I come from Suffolk and have lived in London for eight years. I have a background in classical singing and publishing and before that worked on a fish counter for five years. I lived in Italy for two years, taught myself to speak fluent Italian, and am a lover of Europe. Through Leavers of Britain and my other campaign work, my goal is to bring democrats together across the UK and bring new friends to those who have lost theirs over Brexit.

LEAVE

LOSS

My Remainer friends. At the start of this experience, I was new to debating politics with people. Perhaps I have been a little too pushy in my debating technique or vice versa, but it has meant the loss of a few special people as friends. They are still special people, we just don't talk anymore.

I gained a better understanding of the values and principles of the UK and discovered the desire of the general public to have an open discussion about who we are as a country. Personally, I have gained a sense of purpose – to reach out to those who feel that in times of political turmoil, they cannot speak out about their ideas and opinions. By working with these people, I have gained friendships and learned how to debate.

GAIN

David Isaacs

	teacher
	59
born	London
educated	BA Philosophy and Psychology,
	Leeds University;
	Postgraduate Certificate
	of Education,
	Brighton University
living	Hove, East Sussex
working	Shoreham, West Sussex

text received 30 January 2019

I'm a secondary school teacher. I voted Leave. I believe that democracy works best when a government is elected by people with common national interests and values. This is not the case with MEPs. The European Parliament represents countries that have different histories, economies and aspirations. However benevolent and enlightened you think EU laws are, they do not necessarily represent the will of the UK people. I believe that this impoverishes UK democracy.

Freedom of Movement is cheered on by politicians, by the business lobby, who are seeking to keep the cost of labour down, by professionals and the comfortably-off whose lives are least likely to be adversely affected by immigration. People wanting to discuss immigration have been vilified. The failure of governments to get to grips with this has provided fertile ground for extremism, and we see the far right gaining support in the UK and across Europe. Freedom of Movement needs to be challenged so that we can prioritise immigrants who meet the needs of the UK or are asylum seekers or refugees.

LEAVE

LOSS

The disruption involved in leaving the EU.

The loss for the EU is the benefit of having the UK as a member – a country that abides by all of the EU's laws but which is driven by pragmatism rather than pursuit of a European project (and, financially, is a net contributor).

Democracy will be able to function in the
UK at a national level. UK law will be determined
by MPs and not by the European Parliament, GAIN
the majority of whose MEPs weren't voted for
by UK citizens.

Andrew Izard

	railwayman, volunteer
	58
born	Dagenham, East London
educated	Dagenham Comprehensive,
	then apprenticeship
living	Boston, Lincolnshire
working	retired
text received	20 March 2019

Faced with a simple yes/no and no proper information from either camp, I voted Leave. I felt the EU was expanding and moving away from helping with free trade and movement of people, controlling public tendering which impacts on our infrastructure, such as the railways. This is a loss of governance. It was not an easy decision for me as good has also come from EU directives. Living in the north also played a part, as a visit to London reveals so much investment in railways, buildings and jobs. In the north we survive with 1950s trains, lost industries and closed shops on our high streets. That's how I felt at the time. It was almost a vote against how the current government runs this – divided – country.

LEAVE

LOSS

Having a Conservative government in control of exiting the EU means they are predominantly looking after major businesses and the financial sector, rather than ordinary citizens. There is little thought for what we have gained from the EU: workers' rights or free movement of people and the ability to cross Europe without borders.

Leaving an EU that had grown out of all proportion – 750 MEPs across 28 countries. It is a financial gravy train for many of our MEPs and establishment figures. The concept of a common market for free trade and helpfulness was left behind. Now it's only masses of red tape, quotas and procurement procedure.

GAIN

Michael Johnson

	truck driver
	71
born	South Shields
educated	Secondary modern school until age 15
living	South Shields
working	retired

text received   18 March 2019

I am a retired truck driver but still working
part time as a youth worker and garden
maintenance man. I voted Leave. We should
have left on 29 March. Europe is holding
us to ransom. The more I hear and see
the mainland's response to the UK's vote,
the more I think we're doing the right thing.
Mainland Europe rules us. They only want
the UK when they're in trouble; as my father
used to say, 'Tommies die well in Europe.'
The population of the UK voted Leave,
but the politicians seem to think differently.
The UK is overpopulated. There's not
enough hospitals, doctors, schools, housing.
Our infrastructure cannot cope. I wanted
this to change.

LEAVE

LOSS

I feel let down by our politicians. Europe
is just a gravy train for them, for civil servants
and lawyers. Our leaders are just playing
politics for their own parties' benefit.

Industry is unhappy, claiming that Brexit
means industry will die out, but when it comes
to the car industry, it's obvious that when petrol
and diesel cars are phased out, electric cars
will be built in other countries. France, Germany,
Spain, Japan are looking after their own people
and now we need to as well.

GAIN

Darren Kenyon

	inshore fisherman
	51
born	Grimsby
educated	Humberstone Comprehensive
living	Grimsby
working	Grimsby
text received	21 March 2019

I went out on the trawlers with my dad at 13. I loved fishing. I still love it. I left school at 16 – reading and writing wasn't my thing – I have worked hard, I've saved hard, I've not wasted it. Lads now in factories in our docks earn about £200 a week. You get more if you go out on the boats, but people are basically skint here. I think that if someone is struggling, then someone, somewhere else, is benefitting as a result. The north has been forgotten about. People in the south don't live in the real world – a proper day's work would kill them. I voted Leave and all my family did too. Our vote was a protest against the government. They are killing us off. They don't care. There's no help. It's less about the EU and more about the government. They sold us down the line. From about 20 years ago, we've not been able to live on what we catch. I moved into shellfish as that's more lucrative, but people who just fish are skint. Scotland's fishermen are doing well because there's been investment there. It's all down to government. They have destroyed this part of England.

LEAVE

LOSS

My vote was about fishing. But we're not going to lose or gain anything. It's made no difference. It's our government that have buggered things up. They sold the fishing quotas. It's not the EU.

Nigel Farage came up here. He spoke
his mind. I liked that. We thought it would
take 10, 20 years to get new lads back on
the job, but we wanted to get our sea back.
We were excited, but now I think it's never
going to happen.

GAIN

Esther Lawton

English teacher, author
30
born Enfield, Greater London
educated BA Dance Theatre,
Trinity Laban Conservatoire
of Music and Dance;
Postgraduate Certificate
of Teaching and Learning
in Higher Education,
Buckinghamshire New University;
Postgraduate Certificate in
Dance Cultures,
Surrey University
living Sweden
working Sweden

text received 30 January 2019

I was born in Greater London to a Chinese-Malaysian father and English mother. I moved from the UK to Sweden in February 2016, aged 26. I voted Leave because I don't believe that the governmental structure of the EU is one that promotes accountability, transparency and debate in the law-making process.

LEAVE

LOSS

The certainty that I'll be able to stay living in Sweden without applying for a residence and work permit.

Knowing that my vote opposed the ever-increasing power of the EU – an institution where only non-publicly-elected commissioners can propose laws, and whose commissioners confess to represent 'the interests of the European Union as a whole (not the interests of individual countries)'. This is a direct quote from https://europa.eu/european-union/topics/institutional-affairs_en in May 2016.

GAIN

Chris Leak

fintech

74

born Watford

educated A levels,

Magnus Grammar,

Newark, Nottinghamshire

living North Yorkshire

working retired

text received 14 January 2019

I worked mainly in sales in the tech industry, finally running an accounting software company that was sold during the dotcom boom.

I am passionately British. I voted Leave as I fear the EU becoming a federalised state. At best, this could lead to decades of strife and uncertainty and at worst the implosion of the EU. By leaving, I believed we would avoid these scenarios, while the money saved could be invested in UK business and institutions. Another major reason was to avoid undemocratic rule-setting by the EU Commission, which appears to benefit German manufacturing and French farmers. Instead, we would be able to apply our own rules and laws.

There are financial and lifestyle implications in leaving the EU, but I'm a strong believer in our abilities and resourcefulness to overcome these problems. We are entrepreneurial, and have the tools and ambition to trade with the rest of the world. This will benefit us, particularly as I believe that 90 per cent of global trade in the next 10–15 years will come from outside the EU anyway.

LEAVE

LOSS

The overriding loss has to be the easy
and painless movement of both people
and commercial interests across Europe.
This is equally important for the UK and
the EU. As an absolute priority, the UK
and the EU Commission should work
together to ensure that fluid and simple
movement prevails.

We will be able to make our own demo-cratically derived decisions, rather than accept collective compromises, including negotiating our own trade deals, avoiding the constant threat of having to join the Euro and a European army, to the detriment of our long-term membership of NATO, which has served us well since the Second World War.

GAIN

Colum Leith

	university lecturer, pamphleteer
	51
born	Belfast
educated	BA (Hons) Fashion Textiles,
	Liverpool Polytechnic;
	MA Illustration,
	Royal College of Art
living	Bristol
working	Bristol
text received	19 February 2019

I am a university lecturer in graphic design.
I am also founder of socialcommontating.com,
producing *Social Commontating Weekly* for
over 20 years, a pamphlet I make in response
to overheard comments.

I voted Leave. Brexit was positioned as
a right-wing project – where the left should
have had a voice, it didn't, so the right
stepped in. The biggest opportunity to set
a mandate for our removal from a capitalist
neo-liberal politic was lost because of
centralist self-interest and a failure to
recognise the impact EU economic strategy
had on local communities. Getting EU money
for a new heritage museum did not make up
for the loss of the industry that it celebrated.
It was clear from the actions of the EU that
reform from the inside was impossible.

LEAVE

LOSS   The grip of a capitalist anti-democratic bully
       and domination by a neo-liberalist hegemony.

Brexit/Lexit is a historic opportunity for the radical left; free from the economic stranglehold of the EU, the fight for policies that focus on the redistribution of wealth and the eradication of inequality can begin.

GAIN

David Paton

professor
53

born Watford
educated BSc (Hons) Economics,
University College, London;
MSC Economics,
Warwick University;
PhD Economics,
University College, London
living Nottingham
working Nottingham

text received 12 March 2019

I am Professor of Industrial Economics at Nottingham University Business School, with research interests as varied as gambling taxation, productivity, teenage pregnancy, the economics of cricket and the post-Brexit economy.

My main motivation for voting Leave was the lack of democratic accountability in the EU. Economics played a part, as I believe there are excellent opportunities for the UK to develop improved economic relationships with countries around the world. However, there were good economic arguments on both sides of the debate, and it is a continuing source of frustration that many economists like to give the (wrong) impression that there can only be negatives from leaving the EU. We are not leaving Europe, but a particular set of institutional and political structures that no longer suit the UK. Don't take it personally – it's only the EU!

The loss of respect for basic democratic principles. MPs and Lords voted over-whelmingly to hand over the decision about whether to leave the EU to the British people. Many of those same politicians are now trying to prevent that decision being implemented – they should hang their heads in shame.

The wonderful feeling that voting can change something. Everything was in favour of the Remain campaign: money, the government, nearly all political parties, most MPs, journalists and academics, the CBI, TUC, Treasury, Bank of England, IMF and, of course, Barack Obama. Yet the people still voted to leave – a democratic triumph!

GAIN

Merrick Platts

	financial adviser
	49
born	Leicester
educated	O levels,
	Mundella Boys School, Leicester
living	Markfield, Leicestershire
working	Markfield, Leicestershire

text received 20 February 2019

I started work as a cashier in a bank at 16, as I didn't want to continue studying. I am now a financial adviser and have been running my own business since 1992. I have three children between the ages of 13 and 23 – and my hobbies are kickboxing, watching rugby, being a Freemason and fine dining!

I voted Leave as I believe the UK will be better off controlling its own laws. It is not possible for so many countries of such diverse natures to be run with the same set of rules. I believe the resulting bureaucracy makes everything more expensive and the EU has never been financially accountable for the funds it receives. The reason that the rest of the EU is making things difficult during the current negotiating process is because it knows how much harm the UK leaving will do to the EU machine – it will be the beginning of the end when other countries see that we are successful on our own.

LEAVE

As we approach the deadline, it looks increasingly likely that we will leave without a deal.

LOSS

This could mean the immediate loss of tariff-free trade, making the import and export of goods more expensive, even causing shortages in things we can only import, such as foodstuffs and medicines.

The loss of tariff-free trade will lead us to find innovative solutions, replacing goods from overseas with homegrown alternatives. This situation would also cause inconvenience to the remaining EU members, which would lead to a quick resolution to get a new trade deal in place so we can all resume business as usual.

GAIN

Rose Powers

reflexologist
60

born Spark Brook, Birmingham
educated O levels,
Castle Vale Comprehensive,
Birmingham;
COS police cadet certificate;
police training, Coventry
living Sutton Coldfield, Birmingham
working retired

text received 25 February 2019

140–143

Margaret Thatcher
4 June 1975

Leader of the Opposition,
Thatcher supported
'Keep Britain in Europe'
campaigners in Parliament
Square wearing a sweater
featuring the flags of
European member states.

ADVERTISEMENT

Forty million
people died in two
European wars this
century.
Better lose a
little national
sovereignty than
a son or daughter.

Vote Yes to keep
the peace.

Keep
Britain in Europe

PUBLISHED BY BRITAIN IN EUROPE, 1/9 OLD PARK LANE, LONDON W.1.

(The officially recognised umbrella organisation for a "Yes" vote)

DON'T SLAM THE DOOR ON
THE FUTURE—UNITE
WITH EUROPE

For Gran: | For Dad: | For Mum: | For the Kids:

For your family's sake—
Say yes to a LIBERAL Europe

Keep Britain in Europe
1975

There were multiple
campaigns for the Yes and
No sides in 1975. Thirty years
after the Second World War,
peace in Europe had strong
emotional currency, as
this boldly stated text-only
advert shows.

Don't Slam the Door on the
Future – Unite with Europe
1975

This poster for the Liberal
Europe Campaign cited
benefits for all generations.
'Gran', 'Dad', 'Mum' and the
'Kids' are all easy to identify
with, looking optimistically
into their European future.

Terra incognita.

It's a l̃... ̀e

GraphicDesign&

THE OTHER SIDE

LEAVE

An
Emotional
Map of
Brexit Britain

Editors
Lucienne Roberts
Rebecca Wright

Advisors
Nadine Chahine
Ian Leslie
Paul McNeil

018
Associated
Newspapers Ltd/
Solo Syndication

019
Solo Syndication

020 left
Lawrence Chard

020 right
Cofiant Images/
Alamy Stock Photo

021 top left
Courtesy of
the LSE Library/
Britain in Europe

021 top right
Courtesy of
the LSE Library/
National
Referendum
Campaign

021 bottom
Courtesy of the
LSE Library/
Britain in Europe

022–023
Peter Cade/
Central Press/
Getty Images

023 bottom
Courtesy of the
LSE Library/AUEW

024 left
Keep Britain in
Europe

024 right
Courtesy of the
LSE Library/Liberal
Europe Campaign

025
P Floyd/Daily
Express/
Hulton Archive/
Getty Images

026
The Sun/
News Licensing

027
World History
Archive/
Alamy Stock Photo

029 top
Philip Toscano/PA

029 bottom
Michael Preston/
Alamy Live News

031 top and bottom
Leave.EU

032–033
©Greenpeace

033 right
Vote Leave
Take Control

035
Ed Everett

036–039
GOV.UK

040
Kathy deWitt/
Alamy Stock Photo

041
Claire Doherty/
Alamy Live News

042
Courtesy of
Pimlico Plumbers

043
©2019 BLACK SCORE

044 top
Jiri Rezac/
Led by Donkeys

044 bottom,
045 top and bottom
Led by Donkeys

046
Liberal Democrats

047
Guido Fawkes/
Brexit Party

048
GOV.UK

049
Chris Baker

051 top
Xinhua/
Alamy Stock Photo

051 bottom
Paul Waugh
via Twitter

Contents
Leave

Lucienne Roberts is director of the London studio LucienneRoberts+, committed to making accessible, engaging work with a socially aware agenda, and co-founder of the design advocacy initiative GraphicDesign&. Studio clients include Wellcome Collection, Royal Academy of Arts and the Design Museum. Lucienne was Typographer-in-Residence 2018 at the Hoffmitz Milken Center for Typography, ArtCenter College of Design, Los Angeles, is a fellow of the Royal Society of Arts and a member of the Alliance Graphique Internationale. Lucienne voted Remain.

Rebecca Wright is a design educator and writer, Dean of Academic Programmes at Central Saint Martins, University of the Arts, London, and co-founder of the design advocacy initiative GraphicDesign&. She lectures and acts as a consultant at academic institutions across the UK and abroad, is a D&AD trustee and was vice president of ico-D, the International Council of Design, 2015–17. Rebecca voted Remain.

Lucienne and Rebecca were among *Creative Review* magazine's 50 Creative Leaders of 2017.

Nadine Chahine is a Lebanese type designer and former UK type director of Monotype, where she was also legibility expert and Arabic specialist. She has an MA in Typeface Design from Reading University and a PhD from Leiden University, the Netherlands. In 2018 Nadine left Monotype to study for a master's in International Relations at Cambridge University and to develop her foundry ArabicType. Nadine was not eligible to vote in the 2016 UK referendum.

Ian Leslie is an author and commentator on culture, ideas and politics and an expert on communications. His writing has featured in the *Financial Times*, the *Economist* and the *New Statesman*. He co-presents a regular podcast for the RSA, *Polarised*, about the way we do politics today. His latest book on human behaviour, *Why Everybody's Talking and Nobody's Listening*, is on productive disagreement and will be published in 2020. Ian voted Remain.

Paul McNeil is a graphic designer, writer and educator. In 2009 he co-founded MuirMcNeil, with Hamish Muir, a design consultancy focused on exploring systematic methods in design and typography. *The Visual History of Type*, Paul's definitive survey of type design from 1450 to 2015, was published in 2017. He is a member of the International Society of Typographic Designers. Paul voted Remain.

Thank you

To our colleagues
and associates

John McGill
designer and all-round GD&
supporter, without whom
our books could not happen

Sarah Schrauwen
designer and editor, whose
energy and commitment
keeps it all moving

Sarah Boris, Astrid Stavro
politically engaged graphic
designers, who so patiently
offered observations that
informed our design process

Lorna Fray
editorial advisor, whose
insight, knowledge and
care has kept us on track

Ruby Buttolph
style-checker, for her
eagle-eyed attention to
typographic detail

Anabel Navarro
picture researcher, whose
meticulous searching has
brought the image section
to life

and

Daphne Tagg
editor and advisor, who so
willingly brought time, talent
and thought to this project

To our families

Damian Wayling
Katy Roberts-Wayling
Lawrence Zeegen
Zoë Zeegen
Patrick Wright
Judy Wright

who continue to support
us in our long and
compelling endeavour

Rebecca Wright would
also like to thank Central
Saint Martins, University
of the Arts London

To our contributors

This project would not have
been possible without our
many and varied Leave and
Remain contributors, whose
thoughts and comments
are the making of this book.
We thank you for being
prepared to take part and
for your honesty.

To our advisors

Nadine Chahine
typographer and
academic, who helped
us explain how important
visual communication is

Ian Leslie
author and commentator,
who helped us understand
how communication
really works

Paul McNeil
graphic designer, writer
and educator, who helped
us explore if neutrality in
typography is really possible

About this book
Rebecca Wright

In June 2016 the UK held a referendum on
its membership of the EU. Leave won with
52 per cent of the vote. GraphicDesign& is
among the 48 per cent who voted Remain.
As Remainers ourselves, the result was
profoundly shocking. So too, the adversarial
and divisive rhetoric that has continued
unabated in politics and the press ever since.
This book was born of our deep frustration
and despair at this polarising discourse. We
set out to counter it, to get beyond the clichéd
stereotypes of Leavers and Remainers, the
sound bite and vox pop, by representing
the diversity of views held by individual voters
and, perhaps more importantly, giving people
space to explain the reasons for them.

Our contributors are Leave and Remain
voters drawn from around the country, across
professions and of diverse ages, backgrounds
and perspectives. We include 26 Leavers
and 24 Remainers, to reflect the referendum
result. We asked that each tell us a little
of their life story, how they voted in the 2016
referendum and why. We asked them all
to share one loss and one gain they could
imagine as a consequence of the 2016 result.
Perhaps naively, we thought this process
might prompt empathy for 'the other side',
but often it did not. Instead, it revealed
the huge range and depth of emotion felt by
voters – pride, anger, heartbreak, revenge,
loneliness, relief, fear, hope.

What it also revealed were multiple failures of communication before, during and after the referendum – the failure of politics to speak for and to communities that felt left behind, failures in communicating the complexity and reality of the EU project, failures in holding politicians to account, and failures to reach out to each other across the divide. These failures have fostered and reinforced division – not least the Remain campaign's failure to understand the need to connect with voters on an emotional level.

As Remainers, we found these failures in communication distressing, as graphic communication designers, we found them perplexing, but they are central to the concept of this GraphicDesign& book. Its design and contents have been conceived to therefore foreground the role of communication in Britain's relationship with Europe. We wanted to give Remain and Leave contributors equal billing, so neither comes first. Instead, the book has two beginnings and no end, with the 'sides' meeting in the middle. If you are only interested in hearing from one side, then this is possible. However, an illustrated essay by typographer Nadine Chahine precedes the Leave contributions and an interview with cultural commentator Ian Leslie prefaces the Remain responses. Our hope is that readers will flip the book over, dip into all the content and listen to what both sides have to say.

There are caveats to what you are about to read. While we found reaching city-dwelling Remainers relatively easy, it was sobering to discover how hard it was for us to find contributors from further across the country, especially those who voted Leave. We are very grateful to our friends of friends of friends who helped us find a more representative cross section of the UK. It is also important to note that we began this project in early 2019, with contributions submitted before the first Brexit deadline of 29 March 2019 (the date received is included alongside each response). The book is therefore a snapshot of a very particular time in British history. Yet despite all that has happened since, our contributors stood by their answers when they checked their proofs in the autumn of 2019.

We are indebted to every one of our contributors for their patience, their interest in this project, and their honesty and generosity in sharing their reflections, opinions and time. It goes without saying that without them this book would not have been possible. And finally, we hope it will be self-evident that this book is not about trying to convert Leave voters. In its design it attempts a different type of communication – person-to-person – to seed understanding, empathy and perhaps even reconciliation.

About the design
Lucienne Roberts

The design of this book is conceived to introduce readers to 'the other side'. It reads in both directions, with Remain contributions reading from one end and Leave from the other. The red, white and blue cover, opened flat, shows two arrows in a flag-like formation. The text pages are black and white only, aside from a short illustrated essay in colour.

Contributor responses run alphabetically by surname. This might be logical, but we wanted the design to signal the variety of voices included and ensure that readers felt happy to dip in and out of the texts at will. So, we decided to identify our contributors typographically. The UK has 12 electoral regions that return members to the European Parliament. We took this as a starting point for various typographic experiments, assigning a different typeface to each region. Employing fonts of contrasting styles inadvertently favoured the reading of one contribution over another, so we opted for typographic neutrality, allocating one sans serif font per MEP region. Intentionally, we selected post-war typefaces only, many epitomising what is known as the 'International Style'.

Our selection was informed by Paul McNeil's book *The Visual History of Type*. He explains more about the choices opposite the regional key on pages 052–053. For more about the history and characteristics of each typeface flip the book over and turn to pages 024–037.

The Other Side has two front covers. The Leave contributor texts read in one direction, and Remain in the other.

The Leave cover is predominantly red, Remain is blue. The colours interlock in stripes on the spine. There are 13 red and 12 blue stripes to reflect the split in the 2016 vote.

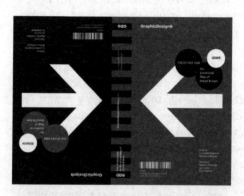

You are currently in the Leave side of the book. Included is a picture essay on pages 016–051 that uses examples of contemporary visual communication to tell the story of the UK and Europe from the 1950s to now (below).

'Telling the other side they are wrong doesn't work,' says communications expert Ian Leslie (bottom). Look out for the interview with Ian in the Remain side of the book. Flip the book over to find it on pages 016–021.

We have used several sans serif typefaces for the contributor responses. Each one represents a different region of the UK. As you are currently in the Leave side of the book you will find the key on page 053 (below).

Flip the book over and turn to pages 024–037 to find out more about the history and characterisitics of each of these sans serifs (bottom). Intentionally, they are all post war, many epitomising what is known as the 'International Style'.

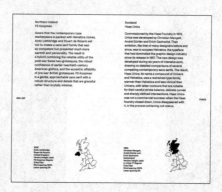

Each contributor has four pages. To emphasise the double-ended design of the book, the horizontal axis of the pages determines the position of the text, with texts rising and falling from this point in equal measure.

The first spread carries biographical information such as age, occupation and region, opposite reasons for the way contributors voted. The second spread shows each contributor's chosen loss and gain from the referendum vote.

Britain and Europe
Visual communication 1952 to the present
Nadine Chahine

The UK's 2016 referendum on continued European Union (EU) membership has proven divisive, splitting families and communities, often along age or demographic lines. This illustrated essay offers context, telling the story of the UK's changing attitude to the 'European project', from the 1950s until now, and the role of visual communication within it. Analysis of the 2016 referendum campaigns is telling. Leave didn't win because of superior design but because its provocative messages tapped into popular anxiety, with visuals that played on these fears. In contrast, Remain's message appeared dispassionate and clinical.

The process of leaving the EU has been difficult in part because the question posed in the referendum was overly simple: 'Should the United Kingdom remain a member of the European Union or leave the European Union?' While people mostly knew what remaining in the EU would entail, Leave votes were cast with multiple imagined futures in mind. According to exit and YouGov polls,[1][2][3] reasons for voting Leave included a desire for increased national sovereignty, fear of rising immigration, lack of trust in the establishment, resentment at EU budget contributions, economic insecurity after the 2008 financial crisis, and the austerity measures introduced from 2010 by successive UK governments. For many, this vote was about national identity, and profound frustration at not being heard.

References

[1] Hearn, J (2017)
'Vox populi: nationalism,
globalization and the
balance of power in
the making of Brexit', in
Brexit, London: Anthem
Press, pp 19–30

[2] Evans, G and
Menon, A (2017)
Brexit and British politics,
Cambridge: Polity Press

[3] Hobolt, SB (2016)
'The Brexit vote: a divided
nation, a divided continent',
Journal of European
Public Policy, 23(9):
pp 1259–77

[4] Daddow, O (2012)
'The UK media and
"Europe": from permissive
consensus to destructive
dissent', International
Affairs, 88(6): pp 1219–36

[5] Stewart, H and
Mason, R (16 June 2016)
'Nigel Farage's anti-migrant
poster reported to police',
www.theguardian.com

[6] House of Commons (2019)
'Disinformation and "fake
news": final report', https://
publications.parliament.uk

[7] Digital, Culture, Media and
Sport (18 February 2019)
'Disinformation and
"fake news": final
report published'
www.parliament.uk
(Chair's comments)

[8] Electoral Commission
(29 March 2019)
'Media statement:
Vote Leave',
www.electoral
commission.org.uk

[9] Mosbacher, M and
Wiseman, O (2016)
How the UK Voted to
Leave the EU, London:
New Culture Forum

[10] Calhoun, C (2017)
'Populism, nationalism,
and Brexit', in Brexit,
London: Anthem Press,
pp 57–76

[11] BBC News
(20 September 2019)
'Brexit: What does
Yellowhammer say
about no-deal impact?'
www.bbc.co.uk

[12] Tidy, J and Schraer, R
(17 December 2019)
'General election 2019:
Ads are "indecent,
dishonest and untruthful"'
www.bbc.co.uk

[13] Adam, K
(12 December 2019)
'"Get Brexit done":
Boris Johnson's effective
but misleading slogan
in the British election',
www.washingtonpost.com

[14] Pringle, B
(13 December 2019)
'Getting a Majority Done'
www.campaignlive.co.uk

1952–2016
Yes or No to the European Community

European integration has long divided
British politics. When the European Coal
and Steel Community was formed in 1952,
the UK chose not to be included. The Treaty
of Rome created the European Economic
Community (EEC, or Common Market)
in 1957. This was the precursor to the
EU and the UK again chose not to join it.

Political cartoon by
Leslie Gilbert Illingworth
1963

This reflected French
President De Gaulle's
comment that the
UK did not act or think
like a continental nation.
In 1963 and 1967 he
vetoed the UK's EEC
membership application.

Daily Mail

MONDAY, JANUARY 1, 1973   3p

A HAPPY NEW YEAR TO YOU ALL

Daily Mail COMMENT

' For ten years the Mail has campaigned for this day. We have not wavered in our conviction that Britain's best and brightest future is with Europe. '

EUROPE, HERE WE COME!

WE welcome this day.

All bygone adventures to unite the peoples of our Continent have been empires of the sword that have been sundered by the sword.

This European Community of which we are now a part is different.

It is a free association of nations drawn together by a common will to bury the sword.

To transform the cockpit of Europe into a power for peace—that was the ideal that took seed amid the rubble more than a quarter of a century ago.

Unlike almost all other grandiose visions sown in the aftermath of war, this one was not allowed to wither.

Men as epic in their statesmanship as the American founding fathers—men like Jean Monnet, Robert Schuman and Paul-Henri Spaak—worked through coal and steel and tariffs to give the European idea substance.

Had we had a hand in it then, the Europe we now belong to would be more to our democratic taste and we would not have to suffer the full economic absurdities of the Common Agricultural Policy.

But these are still early days, pioneering days. The shape of European unity that will eventually rise on these foundations has not been determined.

Today our destiny as a nation has committed us to mix the mortar and help build this new Europe ; to ensure that the poorer regions in Britain and the other countries share in the prosperity to come.

For ten years the Daily Mail has campaigned for this commitment. We have not wavered in our conviction that Britain's best and brightest future is with Europe.

We know that many of you still do not agree.

We think we understand your feelings at this time.

There is bound to be some sadness and regret. No groom marries without a wistful glance back to his bachelor freedom. No future for Europe, however cheery, can quite be made to harmonise with Rule Britannia.

● Today we sound our own fanfare for Europe by announcing the £1,000 Daily Mail Europrize.

It's an exciting award for a unique person—the man or woman who makes the best individual contribution towards Britain's success in the Common Market.

It will be a unique contest. And it will give an equal opportunity to every entrant, no matter what the size of his company.

For the winner there is a special trophy. And a cash award of £1,000. There will also be a bonus prize of a week's holiday in the Common Market.

By the 1970s views were shifting. The European project seemed a success, while Britain's economic fortunes had changed. The Conservative government argued for integration. The Labour Party was divided. On 1 January 1973 the UK joined the EEC without holding a referendum.

Daily Mail
1 January 1973

The British press has always had a key role in influencing public opinion. Strongly pro-Brexit (Leave) until late 2018, the *Daily Mail* was historically pro-European, as this front page shows.

UK parliamentary sovereignty meant that this decision to join could be made by Parliament – its members are regularly elected by the people in order to represent them. Labour's 1974 general election manifesto promised to put EEC membership to a public vote and to renegotiate its terms. A referendum was held on 5 June 1975.

50 pence coin and 5p stamp 1973

Unity with the (then) nine member states was symbolised on the special coins and stamps released by the Royal Mint and Royal Mail to commemorate the UK joining the EEC.

Yes/No referendum campaign materials 1975

Both leaflets (top right), though issued by opposing sides, were funded by a government grant, using the same neutral visual language. The future-focused design (right) was aimed at the young.

**Referendum
on the European Community
(Common Market)**

why you
should vote

YES

This is a statement by
Britain in Europe
NOT by HM Government

**Referendum
on the European Community
(Common Market)**

why you
should vote

NO

This is a statement by
the National Referendum Campaign
NOT by HM Government

YES!
Britain is
where she
Belongs...
in Europe

Build Bridges
— Not Barriers

The effects of staying in the Common Market will be of vital importance to
young people in this country. Our prosperity, our employment, our environment
and the way Britain faces up to the future all depend on our staying in.
But apart from these direct benefits, a united Europe can help to break down
the old prejudices which have prevented international co-operation in the past.
A new Europe with Britain can establish stronger relationships with other
parts of the world.
We can use our joint skills to offer hope to those people in developing countries who still live in poverty and
starvation. An outward looking Europe can provide new potential for them to develop their resources.
Only by working together inside Europe will we be able to preserve the best traditions of European democracy which
we sometimes take for granted.
A strong Europe will be able to stand up to big international enterprises which abuse their power.
A prosperous Europe can offer a better deal to outlying and neglected areas reducing the gross inequalities in living
standards between regions. You will be voting for *our* future on June 5th — don't let us down.

The No campaign in 1975 focused on potential economic pitfalls and the risk to British sovereignty if the UK remained in the EEC. The Yes campaign focused on possible economic benefits and promoting peace. For voters who remembered the Second World War, this resonated. Yes won 67.23 per cent of the vote and pro-Europeans assumed the question was settled for good.

Out & Into the World
4 June 1975

The 1975 referendum Out (No) campaign saw left- and right-wing ideologies meet. Here, Labour MPs Barbara Castle and Michael Foot share a patriotically themed stage with Enoch Powell, Conservative.

Vote No poster
Amalgamated Union of Engineering Workers 1975

Combining humour with repetition, the themes of trade and sovereignty were as much a part of the No campaign in 1975 as in 2016.

Margaret Thatcher
4 June 1975

Leader of the Opposition,
Thatcher supported
'Keep Britain in Europe'
campaigners in Parliament
Square wearing a sweater
featuring the flags of
European member states.

Keep Britain in Europe
1975

There were multiple
campaigns for the Yes and
No sides in 1975. Thirty years
after the Second World War,
peace in Europe had strong
emotional currency, as
this boldly stated text-only
advert shows.

Don't Slam the Door on the
Future – Unite with Europe
1975

This poster for the Liberal
Europe Campaign cited
benefits for all generations.
'Gran', 'Dad', 'Mum' and the
'Kids' are all easy to identify
with, looking optimistically
into their European future.

The Daily Telegraph

MONDAY, SEPTEMBER 21, 1992

French say Yes to Maastricht

Razor-thin majority for treaty leaves future of unity moves in doubt

By Patrick Bishop and Boris Johnson in Paris

OUI 51.0%
NON 49.0%

Lamont hints at interest rate cut

Major is given more room for manoeuvre

Pound falls against the mark and franc

Sweden failed for straying into Iraq

Airline

The EU was established via the Maastricht Treaty of 1992. This treaty aimed to facilitate 'ever closer union' and a shared currency between member states. In opposition to Maastricht, Eurosceptic parties took root in the UK. The Referendum Party was active from 1994 to 1997, while the Anti-Federalist League, established in 1991, was renamed the UK Independence Party (UKIP) in 1993.

Sun
1 November 1990

Owned by Australian-born American media mogul Rupert Murdoch, the *Sun* heaped scorn on the call by Jacques Delors, EC president, for a European Central Bank and single currency.

Daily Telegraph
21 September 1992

In the French referendum to ratify the Maastricht Treaty just 51 per cent voted Yes. In the UK parliamentary sovereignty allowed the Conservative government to ratify it without a referendum.

ESSAY

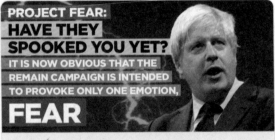

We send the EU £350 mill

let's fund our **NHS** instead

Let's take back control

#TakeC

There were a number of allegations regarding unlawful campaigning during the EU referendum and in 2018 the Electoral Commission, an independent body that regulates party and election finance, found that Vote Leave's spending 'broke the electoral rules set out by Parliament to ensure fairness, confidence and legitimacy' and fined it £61,000.[8]

Vote Leave bus
2016

A key tool of the campaign, the bright red bus was emblazoned with bold white lettering and carried the familiar NHS logo to support its claim that leaving the EU would release funds for healthcare.

Vote Leave website messaging
2016

While appearing to impart facts, the official Vote Leave campaign site employed bite-sized text, infographics and provocative imagery that sometimes misled.

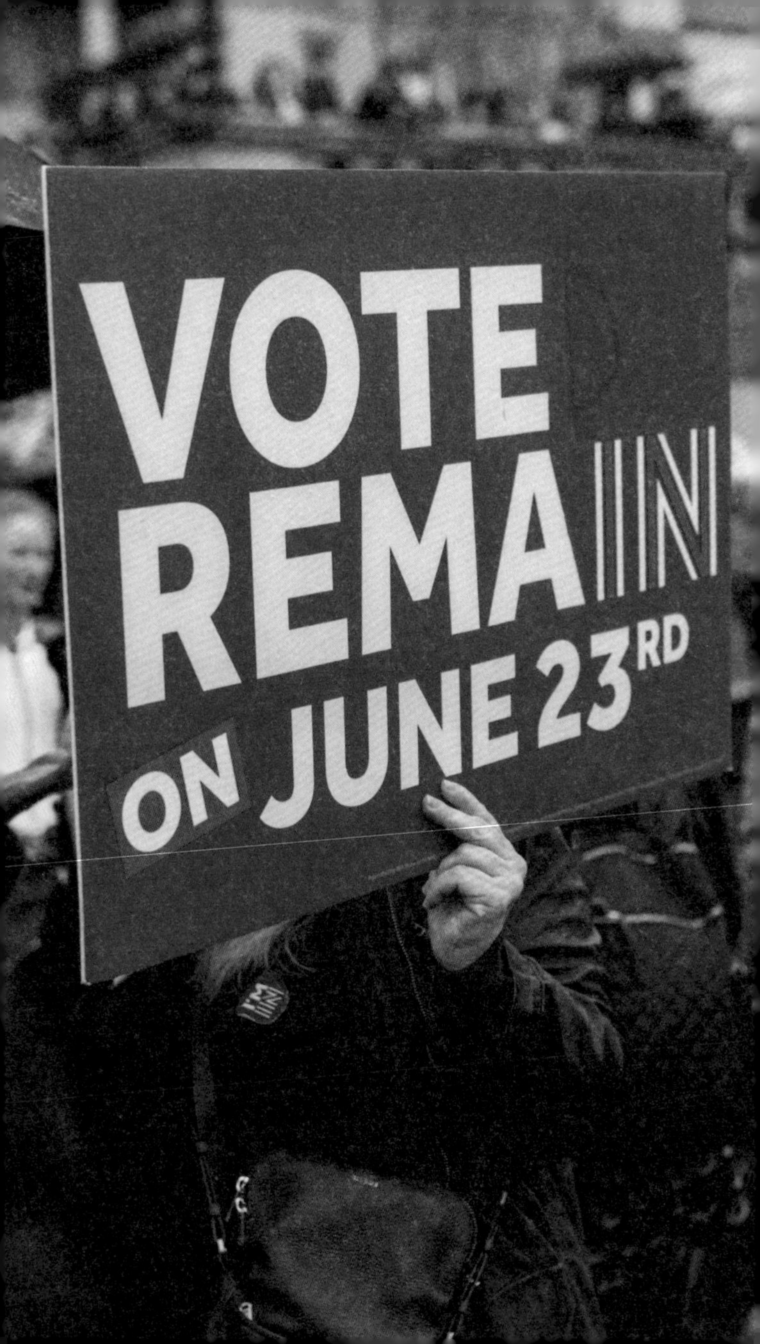
VOTE
REMAIN
ON JUNE 23RD

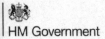

HM Government

Why the Government believes that voting to remain in the European Union is the best decision for the UK.

The EU referendum, Thursday, 23rd June 2016.

Over 3 million UK jobs are linked to exports to the EU

If the UK voted to leave the EU, the resulting economic shock would risk higher prices of some household goods

The UK is not part of the European border-free zone. We control our own borders

David Davis ✔
@DavidDavisMP

If a democracy cannot change its mind, it ceases to be a democracy.

9 Nov 2012

He didn't tweet it, he actually said it!
In a speech 'Europe: it's time to decide.' What changed?

#LedByDonkeys @ByDonkeys

"WE DIDN'T VOTE TO LEAVE

WITHOUT A DEAL"

MICHAEL GOVE

Led by Donkeys
Billboards, signs,
projections
2018–19

Whether projected on
England's Europe-facing
cliffs, unfurled at protests
in Parliament Square,
incised into sand and
visible from space,
or pasted on billboards,
Led by Donkeys' anti-Brexit
stunts have used visual
wit and inventiveness.

Guido Fawkes ✔
@GuidoFawkes

Mad Remainer Files Official Complaint that Brexit Party's Logo is Too Good order-order.com/2019/05/09/mad...

BREXIT PARTY

REMAINER COMPLAINS THAT BREXIT PARTY LOGO IS TOO GOOD

11:35 am · 9 May 2019 · WordPress.com

129 Retweets   **265** Likes

Two parties were the beneficiaries – the Liberal Democrats and the new single-issue Brexit Party led by Nigel Farage (the former UKIP leader). The Brexit Party branding was controversial. Employing a fresh turquoise colour, it included an arrow resembling a house on its side that was also similar to the directional arrows used outside every polling station.

Liberal Democrat materials 2019

'Bollocks to Brexit' was used on T-shirts and stickers by Remain supporters before becoming the official slogan of the pro-Remain Liberal Democrats in the 2019 EU elections.

Guido Fawkes tweet 9 May 2019

As tweeted by pro-Leave website Guido Fawkes, a professor of psychology complained to the Electoral Commission that the Brexit Party arrow points to the voting box on ballot papers.

Paul Waugh ✓
@paulwaugh

Follow ∨

So here's the latest Conservative leaflet in a
Con/Lib marginal.
Made to look like an NHS prescription.
Doesn't mention word Conservative or Boris
Johnson anywhere in the copy (apart from v
small print).
But says vote for "a majority govt".

**A prescription for
a stronger NHS**

With a majority government, we can continue to grow
our economy. And provide more certainty for families and
businesses. That means we can invest in public services
like the NHS.

✓ A new NHS visa for the world's best doctors
and nurses
✓ 50 million extra GP surgery appointments
✓ 6,000 more doctors
✓ £33.9 billion extra in funding

**A prescription for
a stronger NHS**

✓ 300 new MRI
machines, CT scanners
and breast screening
machines
✓ 50,000 more nurses
✓ 40 new hospitals
and 20 hospital
upgrades
✓ Give mental health
the same priority as
physical health

5:56 am - 7 Dec 2019

Scotland
Haas Unica

North East
Folio

Northern Ireland
FS Koopman

Yorkshire & Humberside
Univers

East Midlands
Akkurat

Eastern
Aktiv Grotesk

North West
Forma

Wales
Rail Alphabet

London
Arial

South West
Neutral

South East
Helvetica

West Midlands
Replica

Mainland Europe
Untitled Sans

Throughout
Graphik

Glossary

Serif
Small strokes added to the ends of letterforms in serif typefaces.

Sans serif
Typefaces that do not have serifs.

x-height
The height of a lower case 'x'.

Grotesque
Style of sans serif from the nineteenth and very early twentieth centuries. Less monoline and geometric than those that came after. Sometimes referred to as Gothic.

Terminal
Any stroke which does not terminate in a serif.

Leading
The distance between baselines, also called line-spacing.

Counter
A fully or part-enclosed space within a letter.

054–055

We asked 26 Leavers to tell us a little of their
life story, why they voted the way they did,
and to cite one loss and one gain they could
imagine following the 2016 result.

Contributors

LEAVE

LOSS   The unhappiness of Remainers.

Resumption of independent sovereignty.   GAIN

Helena Fenn

mental-health support worker
38

born Derby
educated BA Philosophy and
092–095
Business Management,
University of Lampeter, Wales
living Birmingham
working Worcestershire

text received 05 March 2019

Darren Kenyon

	inshore fisherman
	51
born	Grimsby
educated	Humberstone Comprehensive
living	Grimsby
working	Grimsby
text received	21 March 2019

116–119

It's a Wonderful Life

As the seasons change, many of us find that the annual arrival of Christmas characterises the passing of yet another year. For some, Christmas marks the close of a year brimming with happy and joyful memories while others remember only sadness and disappointment. Perhaps dreams for the past year were never realised and last year's resolutions are nothing but a distant memory.

Glancing at the festive period television guide, a film that leaps out is *It's a Wonderful Life*, first made in 1946. The highly acclaimed film, directed by Frank Capra and starring James Stewart and Donna Reed, remains

one of today's most popular Christmas films. Although those of us who have seen the film would unwaveringly class it as a 'feel-good' movie, the first part of the film comprises a far from 'perfect' story. The scenes trace the darkness of the leading character George's mood as his mounting personal and financial troubles take him to the brink of ruin and into an abyss of despair and thoughts of suicide. This is a story about broken dreams.

If someone were to ask us if we had a 'wonderful life', what would our response be?

In fact, how would we define a 'wonderful life'? Perhaps one filled with material gain, financial prosperity or a successful and ever-thriving career? Maybe a life packed with adventure, enriched by frequent and luxurious visits to far-off exotic lands? Yet, realising that another Christmas has come swiftly upon us, do we wonder if there is something more? More than we have yet to experience or discover? Is there some other ingredient to life, without which we simply cannot call our own life 'wonderful'?

The working title of *It's a Wonderful Life* was originally *The Greatest Gift*. What 'greatest gift' at Christmas could possibly be enough to lift us from our previous tarnished experiences and reveal to us something new for the years to come?

At Christmas, we remember a man, born in a Bethlehem stable, who promises us exactly this. Indeed, Jesus Christ offers the gift of a 'wonderful life'. Jesus told us, 'My purpose is to give life in all its fullness' (John 10:10, The Living Bible).

Just an ordinary life in Bedford Falls?

It's a Wonderful Life tracks the fortunes (or misfortunes) of George Bailey, the unsung, beloved hero of Bedford Falls, whose every attempt to leave what he perceives as a humdrum existence in this small town is thwarted for various reasons. As a child, George was selfless, risking his own life (and losing his hearing in one ear) to save his younger brother who fell into a hole in the ice. As an adult, he gave up his dreams of travelling the world and going to college to stay at home and manage the Bailey Building and Loan Society after his father had passed away. Despite knowing that he had been

forced into a job that he never wished to pursue, George is hard working and generous hearted. During his career, he is offered a business proposition that promises an impressive wage, 'the best house in town' and holidays to Europe by his arch-rival Potter, who seeks to buy George's business and thereby gain a town monopoly. However, George rejects these offers because of his principles and in respect for his deceased father's legacy.

Noble as his decisions seem to an objective audience, George becomes increasingly embittered, hardened and angry. He never leaves Bedford Falls, is married, has two children and watches his friends achieve 'great things'. Meanwhile, George sees only wasted opportunities and regrets everything around him, feeling that life is passing him by.

This resentment turns to desperation when George's absent-minded and eccentric uncle misplaces $8,000, leaving the company in a hopeless situation. His business rival Potter now has a major advantage and George believes he is doomed to fail, with bankruptcy and a prison sentence apparently imminent. After a storming rage at home, where George pushes his wife and children away, he gets hopelessly drunk at a local bar; he is then punched and scorned by a schoolteacher's husband and left bewildered, lost and alone.

Lost and broken dreams

I think that many of us can relate to the character of George Bailey in this film. At the climax of *It's a Wonderful Life*, George looks back at his life as little more than wasted potential. His huge boyhood dreams of becoming an adventurer have amounted to nothing, while his vision of escaping the mould of his family's seemingly insignificant small-town traditions and becoming something bigger and better just never materialised. On Christmas Eve, after mentally scanning his life, George honestly believes that he is truly a waste of space and he stands on the edge of a bridge and contemplates suicide. Bitter, resentful and angry he slumps his head in his hands and prays to God: 'Dear Father in heaven. I'm not a praying man, but if you're up there, show me the way. Please show me the way.'

A wasted life?

Convinced that he is worth 'more dead than alive', George wallows in regret over his seemingly pointless and wasted life. He is rescued by the intervention of a lovable and bumbling guardian angel called Clarence, who has come to Bedford Falls in answer to his desperate prayer, to show George that his life is worth living. George, who believes the world would have been a better place without him, wishes he had never been born and Clarence grants his wish, assures him 'you don't know all you've done', and shows George Bailey how very different the lives of his family and friends would have been if he had never lived.

As Clarence and George travel through this nightmarish alternative reality, they observe how much worse off many people would be if George had not been around. As Clarence reminds George, 'One man's life touches so many others. When he's not there, it leaves an awfully big hole.'

Fresh perspectives

George comes to realise that although he never fulfilled his boyhood dreams, he was far more significant to others than he had previously imagined. In the alternative life, Mary, George's wife, is a lonely spinster; his younger brother, Harry, is dead; George's uncle, Billy, is in an insane asylum and Potter owns the entire town, having transformed the idyllic Bedford Falls into 'Pottersville', an unrefined, coarse place heaving with dubious-looking bars. The individuals to whom George had given time without even realising it were in a far sorrier state and in that moment he decides, 'I want to live again.'

George finally realises the richness of his life and he returns to his family to discover that the population of Bedford Falls, all of whom George has affected

for the better, have combined their savings to save him from impending bankruptcy.

Where is our wealth?

Throughout his life, George lived by a creed that always placed human need above riches and, as a result, his only real wealth was found in his family and friends.

In the Bible Jesus reminds us of the infinite value of investing ourselves in the world of people instead of the world of money and possessions:

Do not store up for yourselves treasures on earth, where moths and vermin destroy, and where thieves break in and steal. But store up for yourselves treasures in heaven, where moths and vermin do not destroy, and where thieves do not break in and steal. For where your treasure is, there your heart will be also. (Matthew 6:19–21)

It's a Wonderful Life has earned its legion of followers because it so effectively touches upon one basic truth of life: that each of us, no matter how apparently insignificant, has the opportunity to make a difference. It shows that the measure of our humanity has nothing to do with power, position or possessions, but how we live our lives on a day-to-day basis. The film highlights the importance of the individual and that each one of us, being born for a purpose, cannot be a failure.

Why are our lives important?

Of course, in theory we respond to these ideas positively and long to find deeper purpose in our lives. Yet we can also relate to the disappointment that George expresses, when we feel deprived of other people's opportunities or we sense we have somehow never reached our potential. Perhaps, at times, we have made sacrifices for people and never been rewarded.

Jesus Christ, the Son of God says to us, 'My purpose is to give life in all its fullness.' This life is 'wonderful' because it enables us to reach our potential. Such a promise seems alien to the troubled, broken lives that surround us – lives where disappointment and shattered ideals wear us down; a world where many people have come to exist with numbed and neutral expectations.

However, the good news is that for all of us, Christmas can be a time when our eyes are opened to the value that we as individuals have in this world. Here we can see what God has to offer us in this world and the next and realise that the purpose for which we were created was to enjoy God's 'wonderful' life for us. Just as the angel Clarence came down and saved George, so God, who values each one of us, came into this world in Jesus Christ to demonstrate that he loves and cares for us more than we can imagine. Whatever our past has been, Jesus promises to help us change so we can have a fulfilled future.

It was when George prayed that things changed. His prayer came from his desperation, and it was answered in an unexpected way. We, like George, have an opportunity to see to the heart of what is important in this life. We are still alive and can make the coming year a wonderful one.

This Christmas need not be another one to drift past in a daze of toys, tinsel and turkey. Just as George Bailey had a choice to make on that bridge on Christmas Eve, between life and death, so too we can choose to turn from the hurts and disappointments of our past, start afresh and receive Jesus Christ who is 'the greatest gift' and who can guide us into a fuller life, the truly 'wonderful' life.